# Knowing and Growing

Insights for developing ourselves and others

## Alan McLean

# C|C|W|B press

First published by CCWB Press in 2017
Centre for Confidence and Well-being.
Registered Office Abercorn House,
79 Renfrew Rd, Paisley, PA3 4DA

© Alan McLean

The moral rights of the author have been asserted.

**A catalogue record of this book is available
from the British Library**
978-0-9933527-4-4

Printed and bound in Great Britain by
Airdrie Print Services.

POSTCARDS FROM SCOTLAND

Series editor: Carol Craig

Advisory group:
Professor Phil Hanlon, Chair,
Centre for Confidence and Well-being;
Fred Shedden

# CONTENTS

## LIST OF FIGURES

# Foreword

One of the remarkable features of Alan McLean's book is that it provides an all-encompassing theory of human interaction and development. This is a rarity. I have read many psychology and personal development books over the years and they are often too narrow to be satisfactory: The author is an expert on one specific topic and tries to convince us that this one thing – self-esteem, mindset, grit, emotional intelligence, optimism or whatever – is 'the answer' to all life's difficulties.

The academic world as a whole is fragmented into narrow subject specialisms and scholars rarely read beyond their own disciplines. And psychology is particularly smitten by fragmentation as it is rigidly divided into schools. Even positive psychologists who take a broad view of well-being rarely quote social psychologists' research even though relationships are fundamental to their own enquiry.

Alan McLean does not fall into this trap and draws on a large academic literature not just from across psychology but the social sciences. More importantly he does not just look at one small aspect of human behaviour and development. Instead he creates a schema, based on underlying principles which he sets our clearly, which helps us to navigate relationships better and chart our own, and others', development.

One of the things I particularly like about this book is that it covers almost everything I taught in my two decades working with individuals, teams and organisations on development issues. The fact that all this, and so much more besides, is contained within a mere 160 pages is extraordinary.

McLean's Ring of Preferences and various diagrams powerfully convey the importance of balance and context. For example, echoing Aristotle, McLean shows graphically the importance of the 'golden mean' – how we can overdo strengths so that they become not only a liability but our own undoing. He also continually urges to know ourselves better and to welcome rather than deflect critical feedback. The fact that we can locate our behaviour or feelings on McLean's Ring means that we are provided with an objective, and largely non-judgemental, framework, to analyse our own and others' behaviour. It is easy to see how we end up adopting 'stances' such as 'sulking' or 'people pleasing', which are unproductive if they become our everyday way of dealing with other people.

Alan McLean has been working on these ideas for almost two decades yet he manages not just to condense them into a short book but also to make them intelligible. It is easy to believe that he is able to introduce these concepts to eight-year-old children. But a closer reading of the book shows that despite the simplicity there is also depth and profundity. Armed with this book and willing to engage with the practical exercises we would undoubtedly grow and develop as individuals, enhance our relationships and have a dramatic effect on our children's, students' and colleagues' development.

This is a powerful, original book and is a great addition to our *Postcards from Scotland* series which aims to communicate new ideas and ways of living.

Carol Craig
Commissioning Editor, *Postcards from Scotland*

# Preface

**About fifteen years ago I found myself struggling to motivate** my eight- and ten-year-old sons to take up the guitar. At one point I even said: 'That guitar is getting thrown out in the morning and that's £100 I've wasted on you two.' After two degrees, six years of training in psychology and 20 years' experience as a psychologist, the only way I knew how to motivate my sons was to try to make them feel guilty.

That's when I realised I knew little about motivation. I had been working in education too long! I knew how to control, manipulate, reward and punish young people but I didn't know how to motivate them.

This epiphany also made me realise that self-motivation had been a lifelong personal interest. I am the youngest of six children. When I was 16 I was the first person in my family to sit national examinations. In fact at that time I was probably the only person in my street in a Glasgow housing estate to study for exams. This is what got me interested in psychology. I wanted to find out what made me different from the rest of my family and friends, particularly what motivated me to work hard at school.

I was brought up in a family where my father and three older brothers routinely worked a full week plus 'two nights and a Sunday' overtime and my mother always had at least two jobs.

So hard work has always been the natural way for me. But studying, where did that come from? Particularly when I loved studying arcane topics such as Latin.

My interest in psychology goes back even further. When I was ten I became increasingly aware of how my older siblings were all so different and treated me very differently, depending on who else was present. This insight sparked a life-long fascination with social psychology.

My extended family often described me as 'deep'. I was never quite sure what they meant and if it was a compliment. Did they mean I was a 'thinker', or was it a polite way of saying I was very quiet, shy and socially awkward?

I also remember being deeply affected by comments teachers made about me particularly if I admired them. Just being given personal recognition by Mr McLellan as our primary seven class passed by his door on the way to the playground was a huge boost to my fledgling identity. It's a gift I've never forgotten. My primary six teacher, Miss Allan, said I'd make a good altar boy, which I took as a compliment to my maturity and a sign that she liked me.

I was blessed with an older sister who spotted the potential in me to get some qualifications and secure a professional job, where I would 'wear a suit and be able to play golf during the week'. She worked in an accountant's office. This too left its mark on me.

I left school and went to Glasgow University where I studied social science, particularly psychology. After teacher training I taught modern studies in a secondary school. Like other ideal-istic young teachers I struggled with the culture of schools and the reliance on corporal punishment. I refused to use the belt which undoubtedly confused some of the young people in my class. I then worked for four years in a specialist centre for children with emotional problems and became a member of the Children's Panel. A few years later, following post-graduate study, I got a job as an educational psychologist with Strathclyde Regional Council.

I started my career as an educational psychologist in 1982, the very year Scottish education authorities banned the belt in all Scottish schools. They didn't do so voluntarily. Two Scots mothers refused to accept that teachers had the right to belt their children against their wishes and they took their cases to the European Court of Human Rights. This ruled that what was happening in Scotland was indeed a violation of the European Convention on Human Rights.

Looking back, this was an historic turning point in Scottish education. Within schools it was nothing short of a quiet revolution. Outlawing the belt ultimately ushered in a new educational ethos which replaced teacher domination with teacher influence and pupil compliance with self-direction and self-discipline. This shift from a *control* to a *collaborative* culture increasingly placed the emphasis on self-motivation and on partnership with young people rather than blind obedience and punishment. It was a shift which was also in tune with wider cultural forces. In various institutions and in society as a whole there was less deference to authority, more equality and a better balance of rights and responsibilities. These changes were also to be seen in the modern day workplace and in the politics of devolution.

But in schools this change in ethos didn't happen overnight.

Following the abolition, schools had to think much more about the learning environment and the teacher/pupil relationship. Initially schools replaced punishments with rewards. All this did was shift the nature of teacher control. They wanted to retain the whip hand; the only difference being that they were now holding carrots rather than sticks. This was an improvement but it was still all about teacher control.

This approach was unsustainable and new thinking was required. This intellectual void became the catalyst for a major change in my own career. I started to devise materials on professional development. For example, I wrote 'Promoting Positive Behaviour', a staff development programme for teachers. This was the final outcome of work education leaders in my authority had commissioned in response to the abolition of corporal punishment. The programme was ultimately distributed to every school in the former Strathclyde Region and found its way into many other Scottish schools.

I then responded to concerns about bullying in schools in the mid-1990s by developing 'Promoting Positive Relationships – Bullyproofing Our School'. This was both a staff training programme and a curriculum programme for students.

My work has mirrored, and perhaps even pioneered, developments in our schools. It started out as behaviour management and anti-bullying strategies. However, I became increasingly dissatisfied with the restricted behavioural models of school discipline. I realised the work on *promoting positive behaviour* had taken this paradigm as far as it could: 'Behaviour management' itself is based on a constricted view of human nature and has at its core a shallow model of human potential.

This is why in recent years my work has evolved to encompass motivation, aspiration and now identity growth through self-awareness. These developments have all pointed to the fundamental importance of understanding ourselves and others. Now my work is about *promoting positive identities*.

In the following chapters I present my thinking on these themes – at least what my model currently looks like. But first let me say something about how it has evolved. I have now spent 18 years picking teachers' and students' brains and collecting their insights about group dynamics, relationships and self-awareness. I have spoken to over 80,000 people all over Britain in keynote speeches, workshops, seminars, and in-service training. During these sessions I must have collected over one million post-it notes as I use these to seek and collate people's responses to a host of questions about these themes.

I have also read extensively within the many branches of psychology – social, evolutionary, positive, cognitive, individual differences, psychopathology and so on, as well as in anthropology, neuroscience, leadership and philosophy. One thing is certain: there is no shortage of knowledge about human psychology. But I have been puzzled by why so little of this academic knowledge transfers to the real world. I have become increasingly frustrated at the fragmentation in subject specialisms and the fact that the theories they spawn are never put together to help us understand what makes people tick. In other words, no one is joining up the dots and trying to create a big picture.

Though it may seem overly ambitious this is what I've been trying to do in my own work. It has been an organic, evolving process whereby I have continually fine-tuned my ideas in the light of discussion with teachers, lecturers and young people. This process has meant that I have had to constantly reflect and collect data from different perspectives. Where relevant I have refined it further in the light of theories and perspectives in the academic literature. In 2003 Sage published my first book *The Motivated School*. This was well-received, not just in the UK but internationally, and it was translated into Chinese.

Around this time the Scottish Government seconded me to develop ideas in *The Motivated School* as a training programme for schools. I also worked with the further education sector to develop 'The Motivated College'. This work led to the publication of another book in 2009 – *Motivating Every Learner*. Sections of the book have now been translated into Japanese, Ukrainian, Moldovan and German. Colleagues from Denmark, England, New Zealand, Spain and Japan have also visited Scotland to study my work.

When introducing *The Motivated School* programme to schools, it became clear that teachers were keen to share these ideas with their pupils. I first trialled the ideas in my model in Alexandra Parade Primary School in 2006. Since then I have worked with seventeen classes, mainly ten- and eleven-year-old students. In recent years I have worked with eight-year-old children and I have discovered that they have the intellectual capacity and emotional insights to understand the model. This has been the most exciting and rewarding part of my work and has led me to produce the *Aspire Ring* Programme, which can be accessed via the website. (See Resources section)

My final design has allowed me to get beyond the years of frustration I faced as an educational psychologist. Then I always felt I was talking to hundreds of young people at a superficial level, thinking there must be more effective ways to help students understand themselves and to help their teachers better understand young people.

In this book I aim to develop readers' insights into current and future relationships. In particular I present material to help us make sense of how our inspirers and drainers have affected our own motivation. This allows us to pass on the precious self-motivation baton and avoid the trap of discouraging others. These ideas are particularly useful to parents, teachers, lecturers, coaches, youth workers and leaders in organisations. Indeed anyone who aims to help others *become all they can be.*

In the past 18 years the journey I've been on has given me enormous satisfaction. I've also benefited personally from what I've learned about motivation, identity and relationships. And I'm pleased to report that one of my sons has now learned to play the guitar much better than his father.

## CHAPTER ONE
# Taking a good look at ourselves

**Did you ever share a flat with someone who behaved as if you** were their mother by leaving two weeks' worth of dirty dishes in the sink and getting annoyed when you suggested they needed to change their behaviour? I certainly did. I've also spent a lifetime being shouted at by team members in my football team. They must have thought shouting an appropriate way to deal with their frustration and get me to improve my performance.

Or what about the people who open and close down every argument by telling you – 'no, you're wrong'? Or the anxious, over-protective mother who can't see what everyone else can – that she is smothering her children? Then there is the ambitious over-demanding father who seems blind to the excessive pressure he is putting on his children. We see colleagues falling out with each other, each thinking they are right. We know of family members who haven't spoken to each other for years.

We all have countless examples of other people's lack of awareness. And it never ceases to amaze us. But it's always other people's blindness never our own! Does it have to be like this?

We all aspire to be the best we can be at things that are important to us. This aspiration usually involves working with other people. But we vary in the capacities that enable us to be our best within these relationships. What matters most is *insight*, especially into how we affect other people. Insight only develops if we are open to self-reflection but for many people this is a challenge. Feedback from others facilitates self-awareness and some of us look for, and take feedback, more readily than others. In fact many of us don't self-reflect until we are forced to and that usually means we are in the midst of a crisis or have a major decision to make or problem to solve.

Not being able to see the value in getting feedback from others means that we don't learn to give it either. We learn early in life that it's better not to tell people what we really think of them. Indeed we avoid the truth and often prefer to talk about people behind their backs or make sarcastic comments to their face. If they react negatively we can always retort 'can you not take a joke?' We might not care to admit it but deception is a normal feature of social living. How else can we explain the effort we put into charming or flattering others, or telling white lies.

Throughout life we can recall the people who have both *motivated* and *drained* us. These are our personal heroes and villains, and we carry their impact into our future relationships. However, our appreciation of others' impact on our lives usually remains subconscious.

Let's start with how we see other people. To a degree, we can read each other through the clues about emotions and attitudes conveyed through body language. But we are all unique and complex originals and this isn't foolproof. Indeed given human diversity it's actually a wonder we understand each other at all.

We size up other people quickly through 'rules of thumb' with which we 'type' them according to a few key features. Subjectivity is inevitable because we can't make any evaluation of other people without bringing ourselves and our emotions into the equation. Furthermore, as the psychologist Mark Leary has shown, first impressions have an emotional impact and colour our subsequent judgements, and they rarely change.

We need to treat our view of others with caution. We believe that our senses provide us with an objective representation of the world, a phenomenon called *naive realism*. However, we create our own reality through our perceptions and inferences, not some objective truth. Eyewitness reports have been found to be the least reliable evidence in court. We see what we want or expect to see and our perceptions are distorted by our biases that lead us astray. Kings are only rulers if we see them as such and diamonds are only precious if we decide to give them value. Perception doesn't work like a camera. Rather, it works through filters that compare what we see with what we want to see. The filters through which we perceive others are like our favourite newspapers and social media: biased to suit our particular perspective.

The psychologist Daniel Kahneman received a Nobel Prize for demonstrating that we rely mostly on our subconscious intuition and our conscious mind has little access to its unconscious workings. Intuition allows us to make the best use of our limited working memory, by creating habits that require little conscious effort. Intuition serves to provide quick reactions to the challenges we face. However, it misleads us into seeing the world more simply than it really is. So when making sense of others we rely on our basic gut feelings of liking or disliking to guide our judgements of them.

One of the first things we pick up about others when we meet them is their attitude towards us. We then adjust our behaviour towards them accordingly. We respond openly to people who are warm towards us, and defensively to those who appear cold. When we meet someone for the first time, we tend to work out whether they are positively or negatively disposed towards us and whether they have the power to act on this disposition. As Susan Fiske and colleagues have shown we judge others predominantly on two qualities: *warmth*, whether they are friendly, and *competence*, whether they have the ability to deliver on their intentions. We know that warmth can be faked but competence can't. If we spot one single competent behaviour in another person we tend to assume they are generally capable. If someone displays one single example of cold behaviour towards us we are likely to categorise the person as hostile.

Perception is only ever partial. We judge people through a small number of key features. The distinguished psychologist Roy Baumeister is the lead author of an important review paper called 'Bad is Stronger than Good'. This research shows that people's 'bad traits' make a stronger impression on us than their 'good traits'. This is part of a wider phenomenon often called 'the negativity bias'. Researchers speculate that negative information may have a survival value and so we can't afford to ignore it. This means we give it much more weight than positive information. So, for example, if someone cheats, we only see the cheat, yet that is usually just one, albeit important, feature of the person. In other words, if a key feature about someone's behaviour is negative, the whole person is tainted.

However, the converse can also be true. We can evaluate people through what the business writer Phil Rosenzweig calls 'the halo effect'. Here we generalise about the person from our judgement of one or two positive attributes. This is why we think attractive people are generally better at everything.

We trust our intuitions about people and regard them as revelations of character. Indeed most of us believe that we are good judges of character. Our confidence in our judgements reflects the coherence of the information we assemble and the ease of processing it but, unfortunately, not its validity. How many of us have had the experience of someone we know well 'getting us wrong' or, alternatively, of being dumbfounded by someone's behaviour which we judge to be totally 'out of character'.

While we assume that our inference of another person's internal state from their body language is a good way of understanding them, the psychologist Nicholas Epley argues that this can produce more error than insight. We are so confident in our reading of others that we don't bother to ask them for their perspective. However, we need to ask directly how others feel about things, or listen carefully while they drop hints. Knowing others' minds requires asking and listening, not just guessing.

When it comes to seeing ourselves, objectivity becomes an even greater challenge. 'I must in all modesty describe my own person; irreplaceable.' This was how Adolph Hitler saw himself. We assume that we have inside information about ourselves that makes these perceptions accurate. But, in fact, our views of others can be more objective than our views of ourselves. Why is this?

Robert Trivers, the eminent evolutionary biologist, has explained how self-deception has developed through human evolution. Reading the intentions of others has always been fundamental to our self-preservation. But while we have honed our ability to spot deception in others, we have ended up being good at self-deception. So we can convince ourselves of something and yet have no awareness that we are deceiving ourselves: the process of rationalisation cleverly obscures what we are up to.

But while we rarely spot when we are deceiving ourselves we can often see when other people are deceiving themselves. Why? Firstly, when we observe other people we have the advantage of distance. With ourselves, the constant stream of consciousness makes it hard to see ourselves. Secondly, our psychological immune system protects us by creating a safety net which allows us to see ourselves positively.

Most of us recall good things about ourselves more easily than bad things but, interestingly, we don't do the same with others. We prefer to hold on to our recollections of others' shortcomings, gaffes and insults. Memories of ourselves are often stories we unknowingly create to boost our ego and they operate like propaganda. Memories are never full recollections of an experience and they are prone to error. In fact the psychologist Anthony Greenwald in a landmark paper in 1980 argued that it is our 'totalitarian ego' who writes our 'self-stories'. Just as dictators revise history to flatter themselves we similarly distort our past so that we create our 'ideal self'. Hence the common family arguments about who did what and when.

Our tendency to have a personal blind spot also means we are better at predicting what others will do than what we will do ourselves. For example, when we predict our success in a particular domain, we do so based on our aspirations. But when we predict other people's success we use the much better guide of their past achievements.

Often we misread others' motives, because we misconstrue their intentions. And we do this based on our own prevailing motives. Thus someone prone to manipulative behaviour tends to think other people are trying to get one over them, when often their intentions are actually benign.

For all these reasons we look at ourselves in a rose-tinted mirror. This is why most of us are convinced that we have above average driving skills. It is tempting to think we are smarter than others and we subconsciously leak this arrogance. Have you ever been annoyed with someone because you feel they're not giving you the credit you deserve? Join the club! Research shows that most of us tend to overestimate our contribution relative to others' input. We readily distort our perceptions of events in our favour. For example, if we hurt others we often minimise the damage caused and exonerate ourselves. But as victims we tend to nurse our grievances.

Reasoning should help us make better evaluations about ourselves but in fact it can lead to flawed judgements. The evolutionary psychologists, Hugo Mercier and Dan Sperber, have argued that reasoning has evolved not to make good decisions but to prevent us from getting exploited. Reasoning helps us to win arguments and convince other people that we are right. It explains the confirmation bias that makes us find arguments for our own ideas. This bias is not a flaw of reasoning, it's actually a built-in feature. We can't see this bias in ourselves but we see it in others.

When making sense of our own behaviour, we grasp intuitively the power of context. We realise that we respond to people within the situations we find ourselves in. This means that if we need to justify what we did, we let ourselves off the hook. Most murderers, for example, put their crime down to the situation, justifying their actions by blaming their victim: 'I told him to hand over all the money. When he put his hand under the counter I had to shoot him.'

The context and its impact on our behaviour are obvious to us, but we are blind to how context affects others. Consequently, we typically underestimate the impact of circumstances when evaluating other people's behaviour and prefer instead to put their behaviour down to personality traits. As the truism goes, 'We judge our friends by their behaviour, our enemies by their mistakes and ourselves by our intentions!'

The tendency to let ourselves off the hook is in some respects a strength. If we saw all our shortcomings in sharp relief, we might find it difficult to like ourselves enough to keep going! But it is also an Achilles' heel as it impedes self-awareness and makes us judgemental and critical of others.

The positive self-deception mode applies to most people. There are, of course, exceptions to this norm. On the one hand some people push positive self-perception to extremes. These are the arrogant people who see themselves as superior and are always boasting and exaggerating their success. Those who are even more extreme narcissists not only overstate successes but also deny failure and react with hostility when anything goes wrong. They deflect criticism rather than reflect on it and blame everyone else for failure. There is some evidence that such petulant bravado is an attempt to shore up a fragile identity, if not subconscious self-loathing. As the psychologist Jessica Tracy has shown, narcissism is a complex mix of grandiosity and vulnerability. People often assume that bullying is caused by low self-esteem, but it is more likely the result of a bloated and threatened identity.

Psychologists have recently identified a new variant of

narcissism which they term 'communal narcissism'. This refers to people who see themselves as saintly and boast about their superior helpfulness, kindness, and caring.

In stark contrast, some people have a running commentary of negative self-talk. We all know people who don't seem to realise how talented they are because of excessive self-doubt. Such submissive figures are hard to encourage and only listen to criticism, or punish themselves with self-critical thoughts. They swallow hook, line and sinker the view of themselves communicated by their critics. They don't believe compliments, assuming that people are just being kind.

Some people are also quick to condemn themselves and absorb shame. When shame calcifies into rigid acquiescence, danger beckons. The British clinical psychologist Paul Gilbert, founder of 'compassionate mind training', shows that shame can leave us full of self-recriminations. We can also deploy humour to belittle ourselves, constantly apologising or saying, 'oh just ignore me'. Submissive shame is likely when we find ourselves without status and feeling powerless to do anything about it.

The framework presented in this book offers an antidote to subjectivity and self-deception. It's designed to encourage greater objectivity and honest self-reflection and build insight, particularly into how we affect others. It offers a respectful language we can use to talk with the dirty dish piler, the shouty team member, or the sulky colleague. A language which ensures that we can both be heard.

CHAPTER TWO
# What makes us who we are

**There is only a point in developing insight if we think we** can have some say over the kind of person we are. Do we have any control over who we are, or is this predetermined by factors beyond our control? To answer this we need to understand the psychology of the individual. The experience of being an individual, our essential 'me-ness', consists of four main aspects, namely:

- Personality

- Identity

- Motives

- Emotions

This chapter introduces the inner workings of the individual and later chapters will discuss each aspect in detail. The four aspects have evolved to help us feel good about and fulfil ourselves. We will explore each aspect separately in order to further our understanding of their different functions and how they relate to each other. In reality, of course, they are inseparable and can't be disentangled from one another.

The social science research community has mined extensively each of the four aspects and has amassed a wealth of knowledge.

However this knowledge exists in disconnected academic fields. Little of this huge resource has been integrated and applied in real life contexts.

The term *personality* has been broadly used in everyday conversation as a catch-all term for everything that makes up the individual. In actual fact personality is only one aspect of being an individual. I aim to outline the specific role and function of personality and draw out the full importance of the other, often overlooked, aspect, namely identity.

## Personality

We can think about personality in two ways. Firstly, the innate dispositions and characteristics that we are born with which are a foundational part of our genetic makeup. Personality provides the hard wired roots for our predictability as an individual. As a consequence it is to some degree unlikely to change. The personality theorist Dan P. McAdams has shown from studies of twins and adopted children that even the way parents raise their children doesn't have much impact on their children's personality.

Secondly, personality is the presentation of our external self, the part of ourselves that others see. We are 'summed up' by others in terms that capture the kind of person we show to the world; we are described as having an extravert or an introvert personality. These are the kind of terms that we use to describe each other in a word or a phrase. We are all much more complex than these labels, but the overview we have of each other can be captured in personality terms and gives the illusion of a holistic picture.

## Identity

Our identity is our inner self, hidden from the world by our personality. Identity is a familiar term but one which we struggle to define beyond the generic labels we claim for ourselves like race, gender and nationality. Identity is far more than this. It is the way we see ourselves. We talk a lot about self-esteem, self-belief and growth or fixed mindsets about ability, but what is less commonly understood is that these are in fact components of identity. Self-esteem is the part of our identity that values ourselves. If our personality is our means of projecting ourselves in the world, the 'outer me', identity is the 'inner me', how we experience and regard ourselves from the inside.

Our identity evolves partly through our interpretations of our life experiences and autobiographical memories as we form a sense of who we are. Our identity acts like a compass that helps us to find our direction in life and navigate our social world. The more developed and coherent our identity, the more centred we are as a person. This is the secret to the people who strike us as grounded and who 'know their own mind'. A resilient and fleshed out identity enables us to step out with confidence and cope with life's challenges. A hollow and unexplored identity leaves us fragile and this can be displayed in the person we show to the world.

As our identity changes through life's experiences, this is reflected sometimes in subtle shifts in our personality. An introvert won't change to become an extravert, but a career that requires public speaking might demand and develop extravert traits, whereas a number of knocks along life's journey might render an extravert more subdued.

Our identity primes us to engage with and make sense of the world in particular ways. Identity creates attitudes to buttress itself and maintain its integrity and consistency. Although we experience our identity as stable, it is actually responsive to different situations, especially to the people within these situations. More specifically, in any situation, our attitudes reflect how we value ourselves and others. These attitudes come from our identity. For example, if we see ourselves as superior to the people around us, we will come across as arrogant.

**Emotions**

Emotions are physical and subjective states that are our evaluative responses to something happening. Our emotions demand and get complete attention from us. They signal directly to us our needs and then tell us how well we are meeting these needs. Most of our emotions are about progress towards our goals or how we are affected by others. Through our body language and facial expressions, our emotions also let people around us know what is happening to us. Emotions usually guide us towards self-fulfilment or away from things that will cause us harm. Emotions help us to sum up all the facts we need to consider when making decisions. If bad outcomes are likely, discomfiting 'gut feelings' put us off. Positive gut feelings encourage us to go for it.

**Motives**

Our most significant motives have evolved in order to meet our core psychological needs. While our personality is on view to the world, our motives may be kept to ourselves, and also sometimes from ourselves. Maarten Vansteenksite, the Belgian self-determination researcher, has shown how the stronger and more satisfied our motives, the more congruent and coherent our overall well-being.

The table below pairs each underlying need with its motive.

| Psychological need | Motive |
|---|---|
| **Affiliation** <br> a sense of belonging | To seek **acceptance** |
| **Shared autonomy** <br> a sense of collective power | To contribute to a **common purpose** |
| **Agency** <br> a sense of confidence | To make **progress** |
| **Personal autonomy** <br> a sense of individual power | To seek **status** |

We all have the same psychological needs but we overcome our challenges in our own unique way. For each individual, some motives are stronger than others. We will discover how significant our *preferences* are in shaping our choices. Indeed these core preferences form the basis of the model presented here which helps us to make better sense of our emotions and attitudes and to better understand how we affect each other.

We invest our heart and soul in our aspirations. When personality, motives, emotions and identity are aligned they create our goals. We feel good about ourselves, we achieve and we experience fulfilment. Whenever we don't do this, we fail to achieve.

We have a two-way interaction with our surroundings, especially our relationships. We have to adjust to changes in our environment. Sometimes this is an easy adjustment and enriching, sometimes difficult and damaging. We also affect what is happening around us.

As we have seen, the psychology of the individual is multi-layered. I have tried for many years to create a schema that would help people hold together all the aspects of our inner workings. This quest has been challenging because an individual's psychology is complex and abstract. Any schema I devised confused rather than illuminated. I then experimented with some visual metaphors and the best fit I've found is a tree. The main parts of the tree, outlined in Appendix 1, represent personality, identity, motives and emotions, as well as our aspirations and achievements. The tree helped me to hold together the main aspects of what makes us who we are. I was then more able to consider the relationships between the different aspects, particularly between personality and identity, and so better understand our inner life.

In conclusion, the four aspects of self are not of equal weight in shaping the individual. Motives and emotions are the churning internal dynamics. The main players, identity and personality, are two different perspectives on an individual. Personality is the external me and identity is the internal me. Personality is the individual's public face. Identity is the individual's private view of themselves. We project our personality, the kind of person we want to show to the world, through our behaviour. We also project our identity indirectly through our attitudes and opinions. We define ourselves by the attitudes and opinions we *choose to* show to the world. The key to understanding the difference between personality and identity is this; *others relate to my personality, I relate to my identity.*

Personality traits are the collective consensus developed over the centuries on what people can be like. We intuitively apply this consensus to each other and it works reasonably well. Personality psychologists over the last fifty years have captured the structure of these traits and we can now measure people's personalities fairly accurately. Because it can be measured in a way that gives it scientific credibility personality has become paramount in our way of thinking about people.

The answer to the question posed at the start of this chapter – Do we have any control over who we are? – is a key message of this book. While we are born with our personality it is our experiences that shape more significantly our whole 'me-ness'. As we proceed through the book, we will discover we have more control than we realise over the important aspects of our inner workings.

## CHAPTER THREE

# Feel good preferences

**More than anything else in life we all want to feel good about** ourselves. Easier said than done. So what stops us? Where do we go wrong?

Our lives can be blighted by two deep-seated psychological fears. From childhood to old age we dread loneliness – the fear of isolation. Our other fear is insignificance – feeling we don't matter. Frans de Waal, the celebrated Dutch primatologist, has found that solitary confinement is the most extreme punishment for human beings. The Canadian management expert Jane O'Reilly has found that being ignored by colleagues is more common at work, as well as more distressing, than harassment. It is also more likely to make people pack in their jobs. Ostracism, which could be described as 'social death', is particularly toxic because it is such a threat to our sense of belonging. Even negative attention is better than no attention. All these experiences have such a devastating impact because they tap into both our fears of isolation and insignificance.

Feeling good about ourselves comes from overcoming these fears and making good choices. Insight is required, especially into how we affect others and how others affect us. In Chapter One we saw how subjectivity and self-deception can get in the way. When we don't know ourselves well we are vulnerable to making wrong choices.

Richard Ryan and Edward Deci, the pioneers of self-determination theory, have proved over recent decades that we feel fulfilled when we satisfy our psychological needs. Psychologists define a need as something that, when met appropriately, promotes well-being and fulfilment. When we fail to meet our needs we flounder. So our needs are central to well-being and fulfilment.

As we saw in the previous chapter, needs and motives are intertwined. For example, we have a need for affiliation, so we have a motive to be with people.

In everyday life we recognise the fundamental tension in group living between meeting our own needs and meeting the needs of others. These tensions are never easy, but they are the price we pay for the benefits relationships bring us. Life's deepest satisfactions grow out of our relationships but inevitably we are always making decisions about whose needs are met. Which do I put first, my needs or your needs? Our own need to be in control creates a motive for autonomy. This book shows that autonomy lies at the heart of this tension. I explain why our autonomy motive can bring out the best in us and others. But beware, it can also bring out the worst.

The critical role of autonomy is hard to appreciate due to its complexity and yet, the more we understand it, the more we can harness its power to achieve our own and others' fulfilment. In this chapter I introduce an original and I hope a more comprehensive way of thinking about autonomy. The model can deepen our insight into how to balance our needs with the needs of others.

Autonomy is the currency with which we express ourselves

and achieve fulfilment. It is our super-motive underlying all the choices we make in order to shape our lives, define ourselves and influence the things in life that are most important to us. It is our power to make informed, un-coerced decisions as opposed to being under the control of others. It comes from the Greek *autonomia,* meaning the freedom to live by our own laws. Most of us would define autonomy as self-determination. At its most basic autonomy is having the power to say yes or no for ourselves.

This understanding of autonomy is only half the story. Autonomy invariably involves compromise. Autonomy certainly enables us to be the person we want to be, but it doesn't mean being free to 'do our own thing'. The British philosopher Julian Baggini sees autonomy as self-direction, but self-direction is only meaningful in relation to others.

The model of autonomy I present here helps us understand more fully the notion of personal power and also the power of the collective. It illuminates two distinct strands of autonomy, namely *personal autonomy* and *shared autonomy*. We are all driven by both autonomies to a greater or lesser extent. Just as all plants need light, but some prefer a lot of light and others prefer shade, so within our needs we have preferences. Most of us will have a preference or leaning to one or the other strand of autonomy and this is central to understanding ourselves as these are our key 'feel good' preferences.

■ **Personal autonomy** is 'making our mark', expressing ourselves and achieving status. This is the preference to advance ourselves relative to, and in competition with, others. Personal autonomy is our need to determine our own goals and assert ourselves. It drives us to challenge ourselves, to feel important and be admired by the group. It is also the antidote to the fear of being insignificant.

- **Shared autonomy** is 'being part of things', by contributing to a shared purpose. This is the preference for aligning our goals and choices with those of the group. Shared autonomy is our need to collectively determine our aspirations. It drives us to cooperate with others and so feel valued by the group. It is the antidote to the fear of isolation.

Ideas about these two motives have been around since time immemorial but they were first expressed in modern psychological terms in the 1960s when David Bakan's classic text *The Duality of Human Existence* described *agency* and *communion* as the 'fundamental modalities' of human existence. Robert Hogan, the personality theorist, has since simplified these terms and calls them 'getting ahead' and 'getting along'.

In my work I present these feel good preferences of *making our mark* and *being part of things* as spirals that together create a ring. The Ring I have devised illustrates how these preferences lie at the heart of our psychology. The Ring helps us to analyse the impact of our preferences both on ourselves and others, and is also a way of visualising interpersonal dynamics. Most importantly, it helps us to see the need to *balance* these preferences, according to our circumstances.

The Ring also gives us greater insight into our emotions and attitudes. It supports us to reflect on how we affect others and equally importantly, how others affect us.

Each strand of autonomy has its own foundational need. *Shared autonomy* grows naturally out of the foundational need for *affiliation*, our need for belonging. *Personal autonomy* grows naturally out of our foundational need to exercise *agency*, our sense of feeling capable and making progress. We are all driven to meet our foundational needs but some have more need for affiliation and others have more need for agency. This leaning influences our preference for either shared or personal autonomy.

Each preference is represented in the following diagram (Figure 1 below) as a spiral with an optimal mid-point and two extremes, one showing too much of the given quality and the other too little.

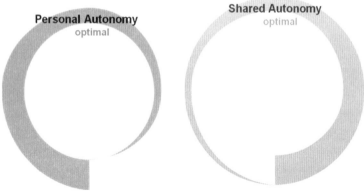

**Personal Autonomy**
optimal

**Shared Autonomy**
optimal

Figure 1 The Spirals of Autonomy

Most of us have an intuitive understanding that qualities work best in moderation, as in the phrase 'everything in moderation'. No qualities are an unmitigated good – they can all be taken too far or not far enough. For example, the intention to be helpful, when taken to excess, becomes intrusive. Or, when deficient, becomes negligent.

This thinking is inherent in the yin-yang principle in ancient Tao philosophy which expresses a relationship between opposing but interpenetrating forces.

In the same vein, Aristotle's notion of the *golden mean* shows that any desirable quality is the mid-point between two extremes – a balance between too much and too little. For example, courage is good, but if taken too far it becomes recklessness or if it is diminished cowardice results.

The golden mean also implies that most virtues are interdependent qualities that shouldn't be considered separately. In fact the positive psychologists Barry Schwartz and Kenneth Sharpe argue that concentrating on one strength in isolation can produce deformations of character. To achieve moderation each quality requires to be paired with a counterbalancing quality. For example, kindness moderates the harshness and potentially devastating impact of honesty when giving someone critical feedback.

Virtues are usually a mix of two qualities. For example, we can describe self-control as 'being as impulsive as possible whilst being as cautious as we need to be'. This allows us to express our impulses when we can, but contain them when we ought to. June Price Tangney and her colleagues view self-control as the right amount of caution and impulsivity for the current context. We can't have too much or too little of the right amount.

To help visualise this dynamic, I have developed a model shown in Figure 2 below, where the two spirals are superimposed to form a ring. I call this the *Ring of Preferences*. The interlocking spirals have a bearing on one another. The upper half of the Ring shows the spirals in balance, where the preferences are of similar weight. As we progress around the

Ring in either direction we can chart the increasing imbalance between the spirals, where one preference greatly outweighs the other. There are two tipping points, situated centrally across the horizontal mid-point of the Ring, arrogance and compliance, beyond which the imbalance of the mixture pushes us into the lower section of the Ring. In the upper half the effect on our well-being and fulfilment is uplifting, below the tipping points it spirals downwards into what I call the *dark side* of the Ring. There is no one optimal point. The optimal place for each person will be somewhere around the top half of the Ring.

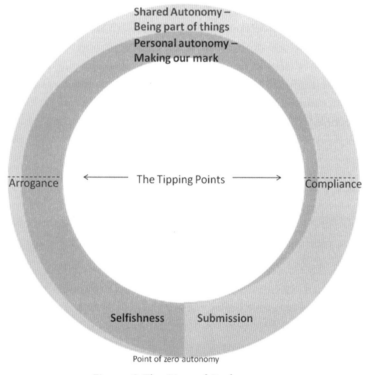

Figure 2 The Ring of Preferences

I use the Ring to chart our feel good preferences – making our mark and being part of things. When both are present in reasonable measure we have successfully achieved a balancing act between the preferences. (There are many pairings that could be represented as spirals in a ring, for example, reason and passion, pragmatism and idealism and change and continuity.)

The two feel good preferences, making our mark and being part of things, are examples of qualities which are desirable in a measured amount. Too much of either is as problematic as too little. Shared and personal autonomy work together and, when in a workable mix, represent *balanced autonomy*. Healthy mixes are found anywhere in the upper section of the Ring but there are pitfalls at either extreme of each spiral. These pitfalls form the dark side of the Ring and are the root of many of our ill-motivated behaviours.

When personal autonomy – making our mark – dominates, it can eclipse being part of things to become an unhealthy form of autonomy. I call this *corrupted autonomy*. This can happen when we have a fear, even a subconscious fear, of being insignificant. One example of this is when someone abuses a position of power and imposes their will with complete disregard for others. This preference can become our dark side. It can also be our undoing as we are warned in the much quoted proverb 'pride comes before a fall'. What's more, trying to better ourselves can unintentionally morph into thinking we are more important than everyone else. Some people can be so focused on their own goals, that they become cut off from others and never stop to listen or invite contributions.

In a similar way when shared autonomy – being part of things – dominates, it can eclipse making our mark to become a second form of unhealthy autonomy. I call this *surrendered autonomy*. This is most likely when we fear we are not liked or we don't fit in. For example, when we choose to submit to demands from others and ignore our own needs we are surrendering our autonomy. In such circumstances we try too hard to fit in and become over-accommodating to others and this leads to submissiveness. We choose to give way too much to others, at a cost to ourselves. Essentially, we put ourselves down. I'm sure we have all met people who demonstrate an almost desperate need to please in their endeavour to be accepted.

At the base of the Ring there is a merging of selfishness and submission that creates a perfect storm of self-defeat. This is the point of *zero autonomy*. It is extremely unlikely that anyone would reach zero autonomy, as we are more often pulled back by the rescuing forces of personal resilience, social pressure or morality, or even by our survival instinct.

There is always a trade-off between our preference for collegiality – being part of things – versus personal advancement – making our mark. We can make friends with our colleagues and at the same time compete with them for status and promotion. This conundrum is at the heart of human affairs and group dynamics and is at play in all of our relationships. Maturity could perhaps be a measure of the capacity to balance these two 'feel good' preferences.

Both our foundational needs, agency and affiliation, have limitations. For example, we might have high agency and be confident but be blocked by an over-controlling boss or an oppressive organisational culture. Similarly we can be friendly, fitting in well and enjoying high affiliation, but we might be there just for the 'craik' making little contribution to the group purpose; consequently we limit our shared autonomy. Without both autonomy motives, we can be sociable and talented but remain aimless and purposeless. We will all have met people like this, and they always puzzle us.

Autonomy, as a driver for fulfilment, is crucial in constructing our identity and positive emotions. Unfortunately it is also what makes us flawed in our relationship with others. We can have low affiliation or low agency, but our deepest follies emerge when low levels of affiliation or agency are exacerbated by corrupted or surrendered autonomy. This dark side of autonomy gives us insight into puzzling, ill-motivated behaviours, such as the ambitious individual who turns into an arrogant egotist or the kind person who ends up being exploited. Corrupted autonomy reflects an inflated identity and surrendered autonomy suggests a restricted identity.

Our most important choices and aspirations, especially our passions, reveal our preferences towards making our mark or being part of things. Philip Rodkin and colleagues from the University of Illinois have found that eight-year-old children show consistent preferences in pursuing aspirations related to, on the one hand, being liked and valued or, on the other hand, being admired and in control. David McClelland, the distinguished motivation theorist has shown that these preferences are for the most part learned; we aren't born with them, and as such they are open to influence.

Dan P. McAdam's research has revealed how people with a preference for control tend to construct their identities around status, personal performance and achievement. Those with a preference for being liked or valued form identities aligned more to communal issues and caring for others. Success for the former comes from personal achievement and for the latter, it is group achievement. Consequently, for the former group, stress often results from the threat of loss of control or a drop in status. For the latter group, as the Australian clinical psychologist Dorothy Rowe has found in her work on sibling rivalry, anxieties arise from the threat of rejection or disapproval.

Our 'feel good' preferences can be driven to excess partly by the fears mentioned at the start of this chapter. Fear of not mattering can drive us to *do our own thing at a cost to others.* Fear of being alone can compel us to *give way to others at a cost to ourselves.* Sometimes these outcomes are seen as a price worth paying. Other times our needs may be so great we blind ourselves to the impact of our preferences.

More positively awareness of our preferences and of our dark side will help enable us to address any potential imbalance. Using the Ring as a tool for self-reflection, children as young as eight-years-old can realise when they are predominantly on the bottom left of the Ring and identify that they need to start listening more to others and not be so dominating. Others who can see that they sometimes operate on the bottom right side of the Ring will work out for themselves that they need to begin to push themselves a bit more.

We have seen how our drive to make our mark combats our fear of insignificance whilst our drive to be part of things helps us counter our fear of being alone. It is when we manage to balance these preferences we are most likely not only to be free from these fears and but also to experience fulfilment.

In Chapters Five and Six I look in more depth at our two foundational needs, recap on each of the preferences and explore further the dark sides of our preferences.

## CHAPTER FOUR

# Harnessing our emotions

**We would all like to have a group of close friends who** support us. People who know us inside out, have our best interests at heart, candidly advise us what we should be doing, tell us what other people think of us and help us make up our mind about matters of life-changing significance. Well we all have this support – our emotions! Emotions, like friends, bring unsurpassable benefits but at times they can also get us into trouble. Emotions can be a blessing or a curse but without them we would have no colour or meaning in our lives. Few phenomena are more complex than emotions, but given their central role in our lives it's worth the effort to try to understand them.

Let's begin with *affect*. The word affect describes quite simply how things affect us. Consider, for example, how being cold or being well-fed affects us. Or how we are affected by being lonely or loved. We navigate through the world using affect as our guide. Indeed we experience affect from birth: babies feel distressed and cry when they are hungry and feel soothed when held. Our brain conveys our bodily sensations, including our breathing, temperature, heart rate and so on in a process called 'interoception'. Our physical experience of this is what psychologists call affect.

Affect is a state of pleasure or displeasure with some degree of arousal. So, for example, the feeling of sun on our back can be pleasant whereas an ache in our stomach is unpleasant. Our arousal can range from high, as it is after exercise, to low, when we are fatigued. The psychologist James Russell developed a way of illustrating affect as a point within a two dimensional space. We can overlay this quadrant onto the Ring, which I introduced in Chapter Three, as in Figure 3 below. I have included the dimension labels I use when explaining these ideas to young children.

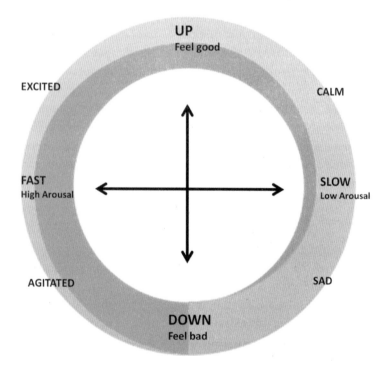

Figure 3 The Affect Quadrant

It is the interoception process which launches our emotions. This is why emotions include visceral sensations that communicate the current state of our body, for example sweaty palms, increased heart rate or blushing. According to the most recent theory of emotion, developed by Lisa Barrett, an emotion is our brain's interpretation of what our bodily sensations mean and so they communicate what is happening to us. We can sum this up in the following equation: Emotions = Affect X Meaning. For example, fear tells us that our fast beating heart means there is danger.

Using sensory input from our current context together with our past experiences, emotions construct meaning and prescribe action. In this respect emotions are our psychological *projections* upon our basic affect, like colour overlays that refine our affect into specific shades.

Toddlers use feeling words like happy and sad to communicate their basic affect. Children don't develop more complex emotional concepts like anger and fear until they are about three-years-old. Before then they don't know what these words mean, beyond some sense that they are pleasant or unpleasant. As children grow older they form a set of emotional concepts through the words that name these concepts. These learned concepts then refine their affective experiences.

The words used to describe emotions are a form of social reality that exists through shared knowledge. Each generation passes these words on to the next. People will readily agree about the basic affect quadrants displayed above and this agreement is the foundation of successful social living. But the consensus about more complex emotions is tenuous. You can put this to the test by asking a group of colleagues for their definition of emotions like guilt or resentment and you will find that people don't usually have quite the same understanding.

Beyond our basic experience of affect we have a set of emotions known as the *primary emotions* that include anger, fear, sadness, disgust, joy and surprise. We share these emotions with animals. They exist in every human culture and are important for survival.

In addition humans have more complex *self-conscious* emotions which are particularly significant for insight as they are about how we see ourselves within our relationships. Here's an outline of the most important self-conscious emotions:

- **Humility**
  Humility is feeling neither more nor less important than others, neither superior nor inferior.

- **Pride**
  We experience pride when we feel pleased with what we have achieved and credit ourselves for success. It encourages us to seek further success. However, pride has a dark side. Most religions warn against the dangers of hubris as a self centred form of pride that can lead us to be 'puffed up'.

- **Embarrassment**
  Embarrassment is a mild form of shame, resulting from a trivial transgression or awkward social exposure. It is an early warning signal to conform and serves as a non-verbal apology. People tend to respond to other people's embarrassment with kindness and in fact embarrassment can engender approval.

- **Guilt**
  Guilt is a private emotion of self-reproach for having

done something wrong or having failed to do the right thing. Guilt works from the inside out; we can feel guilty about something no-one else knows about. We are more likely to forgive or even approve of people who show guilt.

■ **Shame**

Shame works from the outside in and is what we feel when we think others see our failings. This feeling of exposure gives shame its potency as a social tool to hold us to group norms. Guilt is 'I did a bad thing'; shame is 'I am a bad person'. Our first encounter with shame is often at the hands of older siblings. We need their approval and yet are helpless in the face of their hostility.

■ **Humiliation**

We feel humiliation when we experience a public put down which draws attention to our failures. Recurrent humiliations lead to the individual absorbing other people's opinion of them as worthless. If protracted this can cause depression. The fear of humiliation lingers long after the experience.

With each of these self-conscious emotions the self is both judge and defendant. The title self-conscious also captures being concerned about how others see us. 'Thinking about others thinking about us' was how Charles Darwin put it. Other people's views of us are more likely to elicit self-conscious emotions if we agree with them. Praise, for example, makes us feel proud only when we agree with the appraisal. Jessica Tracy and Richard Robins, the pioneers in this field, describe how such emotions are experienced in a diffuse and enduring way and refine the basic emotions.

In the next two chapters we shall see the powerful role these self-conscious emotions play when they interact with our feel good preferences.

Our emotions play a significant part in our motivation as they signal how well we are meeting our needs. Emotions give us feedback about the consequences of our actions. Our goals determine what we pay attention to and our emotions help us keep track of our progress. Emotions also help us measure the value of things. How central a particular issue or outcome is to our identity determines the strength of the emotion. Hence the touchline tantrums from some parents at the side of the football pitch on Saturday mornings.

Emotions have an irrepressible power to communicate. They grab our attention. Raw and intense emotions preoccupy us. Our emotional reaction depends on how we appraise an event's likely impact on our ability to achieve our goals. For example,

- anger arises from the belief that others have blocked us from achieving our goals

- fear results from perceptions of danger, uncertainty or a lack of control

- gratitude develops when someone has helped us at a point of need.

We assume emotions have a specific goal or response but in fact each emotion can trigger a range of responses. For example, when we feel angry we usually want to overcome an obstacle that someone has put in our way. But we can also use anger to:

- protect ourselves and those we care about

- deal with unfair treatment

- show aggression

- win a competition

- enhance our performance

- appear powerful.

Similarly fear can drive a range of responses including:

- aggression (fight)

- hiding (flight)

- feeling overwhelmed (freeze).

This complexity makes it difficult for us to interpret other people's behaviour. It's all too easy to make the wrong assumptions based on our own emotional repertoire. In socially complex contexts like the family, classroom or workplace such misunderstandings can lead to a breakdown in relationships.

Although we might not realise it, emotions are always in the thick of our decision-making. We tend to assume that decisions result from thinking but they are heavily influenced by emotional evaluations. Indeed emotions provide the energy to kick-start our thinking. Certain options will just feel right. When we are deciding something, we subconsciously take into account how we are feeling. If bad outcomes are likely, discomfiting, gut feelings put us off. Positive feelings encourage us to 'go for it'. Emotions help us to summarise the facts we need to consider and without them we get lost in the detail. Decisions can be difficult to make when we lack emotional investment. Perhaps this explains why the 'don't knows' in a referendum struggle to decide how to vote; they lack the decisiveness of those with more emotionally loaded opinions.

Philosophers and academics have long believed that emotions are distinct from thoughts. This assumption was reinforced by early neuroscience which suggested that emotions and thoughts occur in separate areas of the brain. However, we now know that emotions and thoughts are both whole brain processes, one can't regulate the other. And affect is interwoven into the fabric of every decision.

Our emotions fuse together our thoughts, feelings and bodily sensations to create our overall state. It feels like emotions and thoughts just happen to us rather than us conjuring them up at will. Emotions don't follow inevitably from events, but are shaped by what we think about those events. And we can change what we think, or reframe our perception of events. Our emotions and thoughts are interpretations and, as such, are open to re-interpretation.

While our sense of self partly emerges from our emotions and thoughts, it is also apart from them. And we know this because we can observe and reflect upon our emotions and thoughts. As the German philosopher Eckhart Tolle put it, 'the voice in my head is not who I am. Who am I, then? The one who sees that.' Self-reflection allows us to modify the impact of our emotions by reframing events and triggering more helpful motivations. It is important to realise that emotions are advisory rather than obligatory, more coach than dictator.

Feeling 'bad' is caused by unpleasant affect. Lisa Barrett advises that it is useful to distinguish between, on the one hand, physical discomfort and, on the other hand, psychological suffering. It is more helpful to think that bad feelings are actually physical sensations. All animals use motion to help regulate their bodily sensation. The simplest way to change our affect, and sometimes even emotions, is to get up and move. Another example is when we are about to give an important talk to colleagues and have butterflies in our stomach. We can either think we are feeling anxious because of self doubts or, more helpfully, we can simply assume we have these feelings because our body is revving up to give the talk. When we re-categorise our emotions as physical sensations, they are easier to manage. In the example about giving a talk, we can take a drink of cold water and the butterflies disappear, and along with them the psychological doubts.

Emotional discomfort cannot be resolved by rational thought. We can't control our thoughts and emotions but we can control how we relate to them and stop them tipping us into a tailspin. To do this we need to step outside of the cycle as soon as we notice the thought or emotion recurring, and decide what we want to focus on. This is a form of *mindfulness*, an increasingly popular self-help technique. Mindfulness is imagining ourselves from a high vantage point of *awareness* that lets us acknowledge our passing thought or emotion. Mindfulness involves paying attention, on purpose and in the present moment, without judgement. It is useful to think of anxious thoughts or bad moods as black clouds which we can observe as they drift past. Easier said than done, but it can stop the emotional juggernaut before it gathers speed.

Neuroscience research is now revealing that it is not events that trigger emotions, but the way we construct our emotions through our interpretations of events. It might feel as if we have no control when we experience an emotion, but it is our brain that constructs the emotion. Just as we don't simply have friends but actively make them, so we don't just experience emotions we create them. We experience emotions as if they are happening to us in our bodies but our brain constructs them in order to manage and regulate our body. We are just not aware of the process. Lisa Barrett has radically redefined *emotional intell-*

*igence* as the ability to construct appropriate emotions for any given situation.

The psychologist Todd Kashdan, a world recognised authority on well-being, believes that a major key to success in life is the ability to experience the fullest range of emotions. To do this we need to be able to distinguish our emotions, to be able to tell them apart. When we can recognise and name specifically what we feel, these emotions provide more information and deeper meaning. The wider the range of emotions we draw upon the more we expand our sense of self. Making sense of our emotions helps us to clarify our experiences and enhance our awareness. It can also help detoxify difficult emotions. This is why writing down what we feel is so therapeutic. Something that most songwriters and poets will testify. The seventeenth century philosopher Benedict de Spinoza observed that 'an emotion, which is a passion, ceases to be a passion as soon as we form a clear and distinct idea thereof.'

Some people can't discriminate their emotions sufficiently and so just use general feeling states. Such people bundle up negative emotions such as jealousy, envy, spite and resentment and simply label their feelings as 'angry'. Others can more readily construct fine-grained emotions, tailored flexibly to meet each situation. This is like having twenty-four gears on our bicycle rather than just three. Emotionally agile people use different emotions to inform their affective experience. Significantly, students with a wider and richer emotional vocabulary do better at school and emotionally agile adults lead healthier lives. The pre-school children of mothers who are skilled at identifying their emotions have been found to be more self-aware.

The full range of emotions include the *bright* emotions that alert us to take advantage of opportunities and the *dark* emotions that signal that we need to address an issue.

The positive psychology pioneer Barbara Fredrickson, who developed 'the broaden and build theory' of emotions, has shown how bright emotions generate creative and holistic thinking and guide us to win-win aspirations. They also speed up and expand our thinking as well as help us become more persistent. Positive emotions dampen negative feelings and trigger a virtuous spiral. For example:

■ courage triumphs over fear and creates exhilaration

■ forgiveness involves choosing not to perpetuate a grievance

■ gratitude amplifies our appreciation of good events and strengthens relationships.

Threats in the environment lead to dark emotions that demand an immediate reaction. These urgent emotions motivate us to deal with problems by escaping, attacking, preventing harm or by repairing damage. As there are many more ways that things can go wrong in life, and various types of human vulnerability, there are more dark than bright emotions. The dark emotions cause us to narrow our attention on what is wrong. This can make us careful and help us pay attention to detail but it can also make us petty-minded, volatile and inflexible.

At times dark emotions overwhelm us. Cocktails of dark emotions are especially toxic and leave us with emotional hangovers that drain our capacity to make autonomous choices. They act like 'frenemies' who know exactly how to hurt and undermine us. Robert Solomon, an American philosopher and expert in the cognition of emotions, contends that hostile emotions aimed at bringing others down can be particularly self-destructive. For example:

■ Envy stems from irritation that we feel inferior but also from a desire to feel superior. We envy others who have things we want but can't have, like their looks and talents. The closer we are to the envied person, the more intense our envy.

■ Spite is feeling wronged by a significant other, and is often accompanied by unacknowledged shame. It is self-destructive as well as destructive of the other person. Envy turns to spite, when we decide 'if I can't have it, then no-one will'.

This sense of self-destruction is conveyed by the metaphors we use to describe dark emotions, such as 'heavy hearted', 'hitting rock bottom', 'falling apart', 'cracking up' and so on. Extremely dark emotions can leave us emotionally 'stuck'. That's when we need our family, friends, coaches, counsellors, and, for some, God, to help us to 'pick up the pieces' and make sense of what we are feeling.

It is helpful to see that these dark emotions are unpleasant but inevitable experiences. They are like powerful drugs that address a particular issue but come with unwelcome side effects. We are loath to express these emotions because they feel so unpleasant and we underestimate our capacity to tolerate such distress.

Such emotions are certainly uncomfortable but like friends delivering a difficult message they can act in our best interest. As Og Mandino the American author tells us – 'I will love the light for it shows me the way, yet I will endure the darkness because it shows me the stars.' Our emotions are never 'wrong'. They have a purpose and the challenge is to address their message. Where we can go wrong is in overreacting to, or misinterpreting, the visceral sensations and end up exacerbating the problem. Take anger, for example. When we experience this emotion we can get caught up in grudges, feelings of revenge or paranoia. We can feel disrespected and wind ourselves up to feel aggrieved. We can enjoy taking offence. Or we can strive to suppress our anger and wonder why we have such a bad headache. Alternatively we can work out what our anger is about and what it is telling us, respond appropriately and move on. Demons must be made visible before they can be conquered.

Jon Kabat-Zinn, the father of mindfulness, suggests it is not the emotion that is significant but how we react to the emotion. If we ruminate on why we feel bad this only makes things worse. Particularly if we focus on what's wrong with us. We then get caught up in an emotional quicksand as the mind trawls through our autobiographical memories to find a thought that matches our current mood. One anxious niggle triggers another and a flood of worries gather momentum. Our mind can end up like a computer with too many windows open, slowing down and eventually freezing.

We need to focus on *what* the dark emotions are telling us *to do* rather than dwelling on *why* they are happening and how badly we feel. When the dark emotions encourage us to take action there are definite benefits:

- guilt moves us to make amends

- doubt prompts us to take stock and work to improve ourselves

- sadness invites us to put things in perspective and helps us appreciate what is important

- anxiety leads us to respond to threat and warn others about danger

- disgust insists that we avoid things that might be harmful.

Even the emotions that seem to be self-destructive can bring potential benefit to the individual.

For example:

- Envy can drive us to make up for our perceived inadequacies. Think of the short man who envies tall people. He can't do anything about his height but he can compensate through achievements or acquisitions to improve his status, if not his stature.

- Boredom tells us we have untapped potential.

- Spite may drive us to suppress others and accrue power.

- Resentment allows us to feel self-righteously superior instead of feeling inferior.

- Buddha saw shame as the bright guardian of the world that keeps us from betraying the trust of others and protects us from doing things we later regret.

There is also a dark side to the bright emotions. For example, determination can become stubborn obstinacy. The tendency to forgive predicts continued psychological and physical aggression in marriage. Pride can become hubris.

The Ring of Preferences illuminates the full range of emotions and can deepen our understanding of what is going on when we experience emotions. It is in our interest to develop our vocabulary and understanding of the different emotions from as early an age as possible. When we can distinguish what we feel, we experience difficult emotions with more perspective and less toxicity.

We all have experienced the benefit of classification, of learning to identify and label different kinds within a species. For example, having the labels to distinguish different types of trees or birds. This primes us to be more aware of the trees or birds we encounter and to enjoy a fuller appreciation of them. It's the same with emotions. The Ring of Preferences is a frame of reference that lets us tell the difference between emotions and glean the maximum information and meaning from them. It primes us to be more aware of our emotions and what prompts different emotions.

I have divided the Ring into *emotional constellations* of similar emotions, presented in Figure 4 below. The constellations operate in such a way that if we trip one emotional switch other emotions within that constellation tend to follow.

The Ring illuminates two types of anger and guilt. There is righteous (this-isn't-fair) anger versus selfish (I-am-entitled) anger. And there is restorative (how can I make amends) guilt versus submissive (I-feel-ashamed) guilt. The overarching emotions in the top and bottom sector span the whole of the bright or the dark side of the Ring.

It is of great value for children from the age of three to learn to recognise, label and know as wide a range of emotions as possible. Parents can usefully talk to young children about their own and others' bodily sensations and linked emotions as this can help them to develop their capacity to sort their emotions and make sense of their experiences.

We can never fully control our emotions because we can't control the curve balls that life throws at us. However, as we shall discover shortly, we can avoid some of the dark emotions we create for ourselves when we allow our feel good preferences

Figure 4 The Emotional Constellations

to get out of balance. Through self-reflection we can control our interpretation of, and response to, our emotions. In fact as researchers begin to discover the extent to which we actually construct our emotions this emotional autonomy offers us a whole new level of self-direction.

CHAPTER FIVE
# Making our mark

**We all want to make progress in activities that are important** to us. From the age of two we also like to be in control of what we are doing. Most of us look for recognition from others and some want not just recognition but status. Others want even more – power over others. This preference for *making our mark* encompasses all these examples and drives great achievement, but as we shall see it can be taken too far. For example, a proudly ambitious person can become a problem for everyone else. Fortunately, it needn't be like that.

Let's start our journey with the foundational need that forms the basis of making our mark, namely *agency* – the motive to achieve. I like to call this *making progress*. If we are making progress we strive to improve further. Making progress creates a sense of self-belief, triggering 'can do even better' feelings. It is an intrinsic satisfaction that makes us confident that we can complete tasks and be open to new learning. Making progress promotes feelings of *pride*. Seeing ourselves as competent in areas where we are keen to do well also enriches our identity and this can create feelings of elation. As we shall see later our sense of agency also determines our status within our peer group.

Making progress is aided by confidence, something that most

of us aspire to. Steve Peters, an English psychiatrist who works in elite sport, advises us to view confidence in two ways. We can either base our confidence on our belief in our ability, or we can simply know that we will try to do our best. Ironically, while the former appears more aspirational it carries a threat of failure which is largely out of our control. By contrast trying to do our best is within our control. In other words, aspiring to try our best is different from achieving our best and the merit of this approach is that it lets us focus on what we have to do, without worrying too much about the consequences.

Making progress flourishes when we experience a sense of *flow*. Mihaly Csikszentmihalyi, who coined the term, discovered that when we become engrossed in an activity our sense of self becomes absorbed into the activity. We concentrate on the activity because it fits and expresses our identity, has clear goals and provides us with immediate feedback. Paradoxically, it is when our sense of self dissolves into the activity that we are able to do our best work.

How we think we are judged by others has a significant effect on our sense of agency and on our desire to make our mark. This means that expectations and feedback are enormously important.

Claude M. Steele, the acclaimed social psychologist, has devoted 40 years into researching the effect of stereotyping. He found that people who feel stereotyped don't do well partly because the stereotype affects their performance. They experience a 'stereotype threat' that saps self-belief and depletes the cognitive resources necessary for learning. This is what happens to members of minority groups, like girls in science contexts or working class students in higher education.

Three *mindsets* are particularly important in shaping our sense of progress, namely

- beliefs about achievement
- beliefs about ability
- explanations of progress.

There are four attitudes we can take towards progress: mastery; competitiveness; learned helplessness; and self-protection. In any circumstance, people adopt either a mastery or a competitive belief. This determines whether they see activities as opportunities for growth or tests of their ability. Whether an individual has a mastery or competitive approach then affects their behaviour. The person focused on mastery wants to make progress, whereas the person driven by competition wants to demonstrate their ability. People can vary in their approach depending on the setting. Compare, for example, the athlete in training with a goal to improve their *personal best*, with the same athlete in competition, where their aim is to be *the best*.

People who adopt a *mastery* attitude define success in relation to their progress. In contrast a *competitive* attitude focuses on how ability will be judged. The competitive belief holds that you must be the smartest while the mastery belief is that you need to get smarter. The competitive goal leads us to try to prove our worth and to feel 'up' when succeeding. However, the converse is to feel 'down' when failing. Both goals are necessary to cover all situations in life and so a mixture will enhance our motivation. The key is to ensure that our attitude is appropriate to the circumstance.

People with an acute fear of failure may develop what the

celebrated psychologist Martin Seligman defined as *learned helplessness*. Such people lose hope and feel that no matter how hard they try failure is inevitable.

By contrast, some people fear that poor performance is likely to reflect badly on them. They look for excuses to let them off the hook by putting failure down to something other than their ability. We may know students who avoid revision or self-destructively go out drinking the night before exams and then use this as an excuse for their failure. It is not uncommon for colleagues to sabotage their chances in a forthcoming interview for promotion by subconsciously antagonising their boss. Such *self-protection* strategies take over when people anticipate poor performance and worry that it will expose their limited ability.

Turning to the second mindset, beliefs about ability, Carol Dweck's work on 'mindset' has achieved worldwide recognition. Her research shows that we tend to think about ability in one of two ways. Some of us see ability as fixed, as something we only have so much of, and about which there is nothing we can do. For example, we see people as smart or not smart. People with a fixed mindset would prefer to be seen as clever but lazy, rather than stupid. By contrast those with a growth mindset think that ability can be increased through effort and see their achievement not as a judgement on their abilities but the result of everything they have learned. Nobody has the same mindset all the time. Everyone is a mixture. We can have a growth mindset for some subjects or areas of life and a fixed mindset for others. Something really challenging and outside our comfort zone can trigger a fixed mindset.

The third mindset involves the inferences we make about the causes of things that happen. Albert Bandura, the self-efficacy guru, has shown how the explanations we ascribe to our progress can be either building blocks or obstacles to our achievement.

An attribution can be viewed as *personal* (down to me), or *external* (down to the situation). Attributing success to a personal cause builds self-belief whereas externalising the cause by, for example, putting it down to someone else, reduces self-belief. An attribution can also be *permanent* or *unstable*. When we do well at something, we can think we will always be good at it or that our success is unpredictable and depends on lots of factors, including luck. Finally, the breadth of attributions can range from *pervasive to specific.* Some people experience failure as undermining their whole confidence. The poor reader who thinks they are poor at everything is a good example of this. Others manage to limit any damage to their confidence to the particular skill area. Bandura discovered that each of these dimensions affects how much control we feel we have over our progress and thus how much self-belief we have.

*Optimism* comes, in part, from the habit of explaining success in terms of *personal, permanent and pervasive factors* and failure in terms of *external, unstable and specific causes.* Optimism not only grows a positive identity but as research has shown optimists have healthier lifestyles, take better care of themselves, take action to avoid bad events and are drawn into the future as opposed to dwelling on the past.

*Pessimism* reverses all this. It leads people to explain failure in terms of personal, pervasive and permanent causes and success in terms of external, unstable and specific causes. This thinking style deflates our sense of progress and indeed our sense of self. Pessimism leads us to anticipate failure, blame ourselves for accidents, exaggerate problems and draw negative conclusions from little evidence. It can manifest itself in a particularly damaging way amongst victims of abuse, if they convince themselves that the abuse was their fault.

**Personal autonomy**

Personal autonomy is our need to choose our own goals and maximise personal gain. It is the drive to seek personal recognition, which, as mentioned earlier, I call making our mark. If making progress is the rehearsal room, where we practise, making our mark is the stage, where we perform.

Making progress needs making our mark to become capability. We can be highly skilled but perhaps an overcontrolling boss doesn't allow us to fully use our talents. Or, we might just not be bothered enough to develop our skills fully. Making our mark transforms making progress into a desire to innovate and such alchemy is marked by creativity and curiosity.

A common sought after outcome of making our mark is *status,* which is a gauge of our position within the pecking order. Status has been defined as the degree of influence we have over resources and group dynamics. Our status is something we can seek but only our peers can give it. Our status level determines how we present and challenge ourselves. When we enjoy high status we call attention to our strengths and stretch ourselves. In contrast, if we have low status we deflect attention from ourselves and avoid challenge.

A preference for making our mark generates a *passionate competitiveness* and drives us to challenge norms and to take advantage of opportunities. It requires the will to take risks and the resilience to cope with fear, especially the fear of failure. Risk involves facing fear and this requires *courage*. Courage is not the absence of fear but the capacity to conquer fear. Courage is not something we know we possess until we discover we have survived a tough challenge. It is acquired through overcoming fear. This is what makes conquering any fear so exhilarating.

Making our mark can drive us to impose ourselves on others who stand in our way. How can this happen? People with a strong leaning in this direction are prone to feelings of special entitlement. Arrogance, if based on high ability that contributes to success and is accompanied by respect for others, can be admired. People get away with arrogance as long as they keep on succeeding. Indeed we tend to smile indulgently at their behaviour that in 'ordinary' people would be deemed inexcusable. No one condemns the victorious, even if their accomplishments license a selfish recklessness. We can think of tortured but successful artistic geniuses whose arrogant attitudes were readily forgiven, like Steve Jobs of Apple Inc. We tolerate arrogance more readily in males than females. Indeed the arrogant male is the typical lover caricatured and celebrated in Mills and Boon novels. We subject assertive females to greater criticism than their male counterparts.

Aaron James describes how many successful people are not so much wrong about their talents as misunderstand what these talents entitle them to. They take full credit for any success despite the fact that their success would never have happened without others. Arrogant people tend to be divisive, admired by some and disliked by others in equal measure.

If making our mark involves being consumed by our own ambitions, we can become unreasonable, full of our own importance and hypersensitive to any perceived slights. Arrogant people can blame and find fault in others to perpetuate their feelings of superiority. They dismiss the idea that others are their equals and have the right to offer critical feedback and they refuse to listen to legitimate criticisms. For all these reasons arrogant people trigger feelings of powerlessness, fear or rage in those around them.

Research has found that when people see themselves as of higher status and more important than others they are less inclined to seek others' views. In particular, they ostracise the powerless and don't feel any need to be aware of their needs. This tends to be a predominantly male characteristic. Lance Armstrong, seven times Tour de France winner, stripped of his titles for drug-taking, when asked by Oprah Winfrey why he thought he had any business competing again, answered simply 'I think I deserve it.' A misplaced sense of entitlement.

Making our mark and its dark side, 'imposing ourselves at a cost to others', are underpinned respectively by healthy and unhealthy pride. Pride is one of the spiral qualities referred to earlier: too little suggests a lack of self-worth; too much is *hubris*.

Hubris is the state ancient religions condemn as a character flaw, a form of bloated pride. Hubris drives people to seek power not just success, indeed to seek power for its own sake. This is not so much about feeling good as it is about avoiding feeling bad. People suffering from hubris not only want autonomy but control over others. Their personal autonomy has become corrupted autonomy. Because their priority is to maintain that status, they can't show any vulnerability or make close connections.

Such an inflated identity comes with self-deception to justify its special entitlements. This is what leads some of our politicians to take the electorate for granted or think they are above the law, or bank CEOs to cross the line from measured risk taking to reckless speculation.

Most of us know what we are doing when we assert ourselves or use anger to make sure others take us seriously. However people driven by hubris become poorly sighted when it comes to their effect on others. The impact is usually absorbed by the people affected who not only internalise the impact, but also go out of their way to avoid showing how they feel.

*Hubristic pride* pumps up our desire for status. This form of status is achieved through coercion and intimidation. Such people may rely on dominance as a result of insecurities about their ability to attain prestige. We have all met the cynic who tried the conventional prestige route to self-advancement but it didn't work out. They then spend the rest of their career slumped in the corner of the staffroom, ridiculing the leadership, every initiative and every colleague who attempts something innovative.

Proud ambition and determination, of course, doesn't need to turn toxic. Pride if partnered with humility has been found to attract *prestige*. Prestige is earned for well-deserved success and founded on valued competencies and accomplishments. It comes from seeing ourselves and others as equals, from an awareness of our shortcomings and the contribution of others. High prestige individuals tend to be confident and hardworking, but also kind and empathic. Healthy pride inspires us to choose to develop our abilities which further increases our prestige. It allows us to focus on our personal achievements but from the broader perspective offered by humility.

There is a time and a place for *self-enhancement*. In fact, the psychologist Shelley Taylor and colleagues have found that 'self-enhancers' have lower stress levels. Positive, but not extreme, self-illusions are good for our health. However, to guard against imposing ourselves on others, we need to calibrate the demands of our context to shift our focus appropriately between personal and collective needs.

CHAPTER SIX
# Being part of things

'**There is no place like home**'. **This was Dorothy's mantra in** the much acclaimed film *The Wizard of Oz* and it's a sentiment which resonates deeply with all of us. We all want to belong. This need for affiliation is our most basic and important human need. Belonging comes from the old English word, langian that forms the root of longing, meaning a sense of attachment to 'my place', where I am 'at home'. Attachment to place runs deep in all of us and explains the enduring popularity of songs like 'Caledonia' and 'Land of Hope and Glory' as they conjure up images of homeland.

Our first sense of affinity with the world is when, as newborns, we recognize our mother's voice and show a preference for her face. We learn early in life to use our connections with close others to soothe our distress; this is the basis of secure attachment.

The need to belong which I call *fitting in* motivates us to be interested in others. Robert Putnam, of *Bowling Alone* fame, found that the breadth and depth of our social connections are the best predictors of our happiness. The psychologists Roy Baumeister and Mark Leary report that the feeling of being included predicts well-being better than anything else. This is particularly noticeable in adolescence, a time when we are exploring new identities, and when we rely so much on peer acceptance.

*Empathy* is the key emotion that helps us in our quest to develop relationships and find a sense of belonging. It lets us tune into what someone else is thinking or feeling and respond appropriately. This allows us to connect with others. Simon Baron-Cohen, the renowned expert in autism, has shown that most of us show moderate rather than high levels of empathy. This suggests that moderate empathy levels are most adaptive, or best for human beings. We shall find out later why that should be the case.

Because it is so fundamental, empathy emerges early in life. From birth, infants feel distress at the cries of others. By 16 months, toddlers try to relieve others' distress. By 30 months they will go out of their way to be helpful to others. When we empathise with another person's distress their problems can appear lessened, as in the maxim – 'A problem shared is a problem halved.' Equally, when we empathise with another person's success, their feelings of pride expand.

A sense of belonging to an organisation or group builds identification with its values. However, we can belong to a group without contributing much to the group's goals. It is only when we choose to contribute to the purpose of the group that affiliation matures into *shared autonomy*. We then feel valued, not just accepted. Shared autonomy allows us to build coalitions, through which we develop a common purpose that further deepens our sense of belonging. How much we are willing, able and allowed to commit to the shared task will determine the extent of our shared autonomy.

Our need for shared autonomy, which I call *being part of*

*things,* drives us to contribute to something larger than ourselves and achieve success that we couldn't achieve on our own. Think about the joyful commitment shown by the volunteers at the London Olympics in 2014. Stephen Reicher, Professor of Social Psychology at St Andrew's University, reckons that when people see themselves as sharing group membership with others, they want to participate in the activities that are relevant to that group identity. Reicher believes that this sense of community constitutes much of what we live for and what we live by.

Our level of commitment to a common purpose determines how much we are willing to contribute. The need to belong and fit in encourages self-control, as we realise we have to control ourselves to be accepted. Being part of things also motivates us to rein in selfish instincts by subsuming our self-interests into our group's interests. It allows us collectively to shape our lives rather than submit to externally imposed rules.

The evolutionary biologist Martin Nowak contends that our survival is more ensured when we are part of a group rather than acting as lone individuals. In this respect cooperation is a form of enlightened self-interest. Cooperation with others also builds collective resilience, as acknowledged in the motto 'Together we stand, divided we fall.' Consequently, groups with a strong team spirit are more likely to outshine their rivals. Cooperation happens when people choose to work together within self-directed relationships. Cooperation is much less controllable than compliance or competition. It is less structured and can only be determined autonomously by all participants.

Being part of things creates what Alexis de Tocqueville in the nineteenth century and Robert Putnam in the twentieth century described as 'social capital'. This refers both to important networks of social connections and a collective trustworthiness. This is what turns a collection of individuals into a cohesive group with a clear sense of purpose. It creates a collective energy. It produces thinking about *we* and not just *I*. Social capital has been found to be the key feature of organisational culture that determines the success of any innovation.

People with a strong preference for being part of things choose to accommodate to others' needs. They are other-focused (allocentric), open to others' ideas and opinions and willing to serve when necessary. Think of the members of professional cycling teams where everyone fulfils a specific role. To support the leader, whose job it is to move to the front and win the race, there are 'domestiques' who shelter the team leader from the wind, fall back to collect water and food and hand over their bicycle if the leader's bike fails. There is also the 'lead-out man' who forces his way to the front with the leader in his slipstream. This other-centredness holds the group together to achieve its goals. Members of successful teams build lifelong allegiances that inspire camaraderie fifty years later.

Being part of things both nurtures and requires a willingness to match others' contributions and do one another favours, but to do so without keeping a score. It is dependent on the ability to share with others for mutual benefit. High performing teams consist of people who can appreciate one another's strengths and weaknesses, help the team get beyond superficial relation-ships and face up to conflict. This requires the capacity to work out who is trustworthy.

Being part of things also benefits from and generates certain emotions. As well as work out whom we can trust, we need to build trust in others. If trust is breached we have to work hard to reinstate it. We have *restoring* emotions that help us achieve this. Guilt often gets an unfairly bad press, but it acts as a guide to restoring balance following a transgression of our moral code. We also experience moderate shame when we think we have let others down, but still want to be part of things and seek forgiveness. It is an emotional form of apology that makes us acquiesce in order to dampen the anger of others. The French philosopher Jean Paul Sartre called these emotions 'self-reproaching' emotions and he believed that we achieve a heightened awareness of ourselves through these powerful emotions.

A reasonable level of compliance is essential for social cohesion. Voluntary compliance beyond what is required – going the extra mile – plays a key role in life. We all know what happens when air traffic controllers or junior doctors decide to work to rule, to do only what their job formally requires. Chaos ensues. Most of us, in fact, routinely accommodate beyond what is formally required.

Being accommodating is not weakness. Obliging people will usually have a sticking point, a line beyond which they will not cross. Compliance is a by-product of a balanced relationship where we choose to obey because we identify with the authority figure whilst retaining respect for ourselves. Compliance should always be in our own interests or some wider collective purpose. If it is not, it is blind obedience.

However, some people with a strong preference for being part of things (rather than making their mark) can become vulnerable to over-compliance. This is when they *surrender* their autonomy. This then takes them beyond the tipping point where being part of things goes too far and puts self-respect at risk.

This can happen when the boundaries between self and others become blurred, when individuals blend in rather than work out their own opinions. Over time this erodes their identity. There is a positive aspect to compliance as part of affiliation. But a deflated sense of self underpins submission. Emotions like sadness, doubt, frustration with self, guilt and shame push people to retreat within themselves, conserve energy and assess what is happening. Others usually pick up on these emotions seeing that the person needs help and reassurance.

Surrendered autonomy is dramatically illustrated by people who, when accused and under cross-examination, make a false confession to comply with their accusers. They give up the struggle of trying to prove their innocence, as they are so vulnerable to pressure from others.

Paradoxically, the more individuals give way to others the more they become a burden as they leave peers either feeling responsible for them or annoyed. Just as we detest being imposed upon by overbearing people we also recoil from over-accommodating individuals. Both are unhelpful in groups and bring out the worst in us.

Where does this leave self-sacrifice? We need to distinguish between virtuous and submissive self-sacrifice. Virtuous self-sacrifice is heroic. Think of the mother who chooses to sacrifice herself for her children or the soldier who risks his life for his peers. Such self-sacrifice reflects humanity at its finest. Submiss-ive self-sacrifice, in contrast, is a negation of self and occurs when people sacrifice themselves for little benefit to anyone, thinking – 'I don't matter'. Such action is often motivated by the 'disease to please' and is likely to happen when people swallow, hook, line and sinker, any critical view of themselves communicated by other people. The submissive person relinquishes personal responsibility and fails to look after themselves.

The submissive figure is hard to encourage because they have disconnected from any self-worth, only listening to criticism or punishing themselves with self-critical thoughts. The boss who works late every evening, who goes into the office at the week-end, and who feels guilty about having time off is not contributing to the success of the organisation; quite the reverse.

Submission coexists with coercion; puppets need puppet masters. Hierarchies are not determined by dominance alone, they also require submission. For every narcissist bully there are lots of hidden victims. Narcissists are adept at pulling the wool over people's eyes. Most victims assume they will not be listened to never mind believed, so they tend to keep quiet. Of course, experience shows that this is not irrational or unreasonable. The low conversion rate of rape allegations into court cases is an example of this. Ongoing abuse further undermines the victim to the extent that they come to believe they are insignificant and unworthy of respect.

Why is it so easy for kind people to become exploited? The two sides of *altruism* may help explain how this can happen. Healthy altruism occurs when we deliberately act to benefit others even though it may not be in our own self-interest. It is powered by respect for both self and others. It requires empathy. If someone is sad, we are sad. Nancy Eisenberg, at the Centre for Compassion and Altruism Research at Stanford University, views such other-oriented feelings of concern as the 'emotional push' towards altruism. However, to live for others can be a dangerous mission. It can become pathological altruism. So where should we draw the line? We cannot afford to ignore our own needs. It is good to be kind but we need to choose to give wisely. It is also good to forgive but we can be too forgiving. For example, spouses who repeatedly forgive their partner's aggression are likely to continue to receive more abuse.

Restorative emotions can also be taken too far. If we cannot make amends, we punish ourselves. Without resolution, guilt can fester and turn into *shame*. Shame can be useful as it encourages change but the British psychotherapist Paul Gilbert has shown how danger beckons when shame calcifies into submission. Some people are quick to condemn themselves and absorb shame. When we don't measure up in areas that are really important to us, like being a good parent, we can feel ashamed. Our introspection can then turn into rumination, a huge barrier to insight. Rumination makes us less accurate in identifying our emotions. We are too focused on the problem and miss the bigger picture. It also makes us resistant to feed-back. Shame can leave us full of self-recriminations, deploying humour to belittle ourselves, constantly apologising or saying, 'Oh just ignore me.' It can set up cycles of increasing submission that lead to further rejection.

Submissive unresolved shame is most likely when we find ourselves trapped in unwanted low status, when we feel powerless. Child sexual abuse victims talk of how their shame lasts forever. Victims of rape are never responsible for their abuse yet the stain of it can remain a burden, their identity forever tainted.

Feeling unhappy about being put down is the key factor that erodes identity. An inferior position that is actually preferred and consciously chosen isn't damaging to our well-being. For example, some men are quite happy for their wives to buy their clothes and dress them. Some people are happy to sit quietly in a group and not draw attention to themselves. It is the resented and unchosen nature of submission that seems to be crucial in undermining any sense of fulfilment.

Pathological altruism occurs in a submissive person when festering guilt is mixed with unresolved shame. It starts with trying too hard to please. When we are submissive we communicate a sense of inferiority. We gratify others' wishes rather than our own and trust someone else's thinking more than our own. We don't make choices for ourselves and don't develop and grow. Such submission communicates a sense of anxiety about not fitting in. Being overly trusting can also lead kind people to become a proverbial doormat. By seeing the best in everyone and being poor at spotting the wolf dressed in sheep's clothing, they risk being taken advantage of. Pleasing everyone is an unattainable goal which can lead to depression, if we can't give up on it.

It can get worse. If the individual judges themselves as responsible for a problem they can derive a perverse satisfaction from their own suffering and fool themselves into thinking it will benefit others. These are the people who enjoy being martyrs. People can also over-identify with others' distress and make things worse. Indeed some people are at their most dangerous when trying to be helpful. They don't know when to stop giving and they can end up just as trapped as the people they are trying to help. Any help offered is likely to be uncalled for or of little benefit. But they persist despite feeling aggrieved by the lack of thanks. Invariably they end up exhausted, resentful and disillusioned.

The key emotional driver of making our mark is pride. For being part of things it is *compassion*. Compassion functions at a deeper level than empathy. It cements feelings of similarity between ourselves and others, particularly the vulnerable. Compassion triggers attempts to alleviate another's suffering. Most importantly, compassion doesn't carry the potential danger of empathy, namely the distress of others overwhelming us. When we are compassionate we choose to help. Our own distress doesn't overwhelm us and we refrain from being an emotional sponge. Maintaining a boundary between ourselves and the distressed person creates a healthy altruism which helps buffer us against pathological altruism and burn out. Compassion also means being compassionate towards ourselves and is a powerful balancing emotion and the antidote to submission.

CHAPTER SEVEN
# Two sides of us

**We saw earlier in Chapter Four the way our emotions** determine how we experience the flow of our life moment by moment. So what shapes us in the long term, year by year? To answer this we need to look at the twin processes of personal development, namely personality and identity.

**Personality**

Let's start the discussion with personality. Personality is used here to describe two aspects of our individuality. Firstly, personality is our inherited traits that predispose us to behave in characteristic ways, how our brain is wired. We first see an individual's personality in their infant temperament.

When we meet up with people we haven't seen for a long time, we are often struck by how little they have changed. Personality is what makes our presentation relatively enduring. However, personality is not set in stone. Albert Bandura has proposed that personalities and environments mutually shape one another through a process of *reciprocal determinism*. Personality traits elicit reactions from others that magnify these traits. For example, colleagues of disagreeable extraverts may become hostile to them leading to these individuals becoming more disagreeable. On the other hand, colleagues who are conscientious and agreeable evoke positive responses which reinforce their natural tendency to be obliging.

Personality is thought to be innate, but innate doesn't mean fixed, it means organised in advance. We are born with what Jonathan Haidt has called a 'first draft' of our personality that gets revised by our experiences and by feedback. While a predisposition like shyness has genetic roots, becomes evident in the first year of life and is still apparent in adulthood, parents can help reduce the impact of young people's timidity by not over-protecting them.

Secondly, personality is how we present ourselves to the world. It is how we sum each other up. We quickly form an impression intuitively about an individual's personality, based on snapshots of their behaviour. We then look for evidence to justify this opinion. We judge the specifics about the person in the light of the whole. Consider how we so freely and confidently express our views about the personalities of public figures, based on a mere glimpse of their behaviour through the media.

When weighing others up we attribute qualities to them in order to make them more predictable. Having noticed one key characteristic we then expect other qualities that go along with that feature. We assume that certain traits go together. For example, modesty goes with empathy while liveliness sits with sociability. These thumbnail qualities allow us to summarise one another's different personalities.

Personality traits lead us to respond in certain ways under certain circumstances. McCrae and Costa, key figures in personality psychology over the last 30 years, have identified five broad traits, known as the 'Big 5', which we use to describe personality. These are openness, conscientiousness, extraversion, agreeableness and neuroticism, known as 'OCEAN'.

■ Openness to experience means being reflective, creative, unconventional, willing to question authority and champion change. People high in openness look for opportunities for self-expression. Openness includes receptivity to our emotions and is similar to emotional intelligence. It enhances our capacity to self-reflect.

■ Conscientiousness implies self-disciplined efforts to achieve. It is an umbrella term for being efficient, purposeful, goal-oriented and responsible. It predicts a wide range of outcomes such as academic attainment and stability. Girls gain higher grades than boys, even though they don't outperform boys on intelligence tests, and it is thought that girls' higher levels of conscientiousness explains this gender gap.

■ Extraversion indicates the extent to which we are energised by external stimulation. Extraversion is seen in people who are ambitious, active and competitive and enjoy high arousal emotions. Low levels of extraversion (introversion) is the preference for internal stimulation. Introverted people are more reflective, less outgoing socially and more likely to think carefully about the consequences of their actions. They can energise themselves without the stimulation of other people.

■ Agreeableness involves being respectful, empathic and trusting. Agreeable people pay attention to how others are feeling, are quick to forgive and slow to anger. Agreeableness is the trait most influenced by experience. It dips temporarily at puberty.

■ Neuroticism is the tendency to experience negative emotions. People high in neuroticism are more likely to be distressed by the strains of life. It is the trait most shaped by our genes. Interestingly Avshalom Caspi, the Israeli psychologist, has found high neuroticism to be at the root of most psychiatric problems. It is also the trait that responds best to therapy. As a general trend, most of us become less neurotic as we get older.

Certain traits lean individuals towards being part of things while other traits dispose people towards making our mark. Those high in agreeableness are likely to prefer being part of things. Certain aspects of conscientiousness including keeping promises and doing our fair share are also ingredients of being part of things. In contrast, those high in extraversion tend towards making our mark. Openness can take us in either direction. Neuroticism pulls us into the dark side of the Ring. Neurotic extraverts who are low on agreeableness are more likely to show corrupted autonomy. Agreeable but neurotic introverts tend towards surrendered autonomy.

As well as traits, we sort people through personality 'types'. We can think of personality in terms of three broad types, namely:

- adaptive

- cautious

- impulsive.

Our personality is shaped significantly by our *self-control*, the capacity to regulate our emotions and be able to stop doing something when we need to. Walter Mischel, the American personality theorist, has portrayed self-control as the balancing of two competing tendencies, 'cool' caution and 'hot' impulsivity.

There is nothing wrong with being cautious or impulsive and each has distinct advantages depending on the situation we are in. The Aristotelian perspective discussed earlier recognises that we can have too much of a good thing and that virtues are those which are halfway between too much and too little. We saw how optimal self-control is being as impulsive as possible whilst being as cautious as we need to be. This allows us to express our impulses when appropriate but contain them when we ought to. June Price Tangney sees optimal self-control as the right amount for the current context, and we can't have too much of the right amount. If caution is taken too far and not balanced by some degree of impulsivity, it will eventually end up becoming paralysis. In the same way impulsivity, if taken too far and not checked by some measure of caution, will become recklessness. See Figure 5 below.

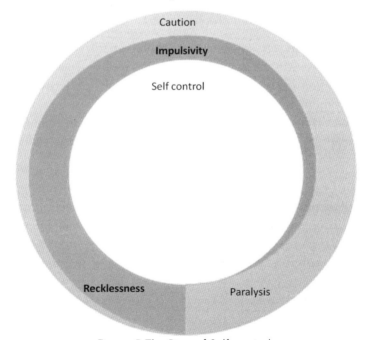

Figure 5 The Ring of Self-control

### Personality and Identity

Personality is important. It is a strong predictor of well-being. However, Dan McAdams believes that our goals and aspirations are only weakly determined by our personality. It certainly helps when our aspirations suit our personality but when it comes to our aspirations, our *identity* is far more important. Indeed for personal growth in general, identity is the more significant process.

The more I thought of the tree metaphor, the more I realised the significance of the difference between personality and identity. This difference is particularly important in understanding how we can best help other people's development. If personality is the outer-me, identity is the inner-me. Identity is the key to personal growth. It is the *story* we tell ourselves. Identity gives us our individual essence.

Personality sets our general disposition towards certain types of experiences, for example to be active or self-contained, but it doesn't determine what we do. Personality traits are not driving motives and neither do they affect our motives that much. Impulsive people make quick decisions and cautious people are hesitant, no matter what they aspire to do.

Personality is the veneer, our presentation and packaging. We are often shocked to hear of the inner turmoil going on in the minds of people who are outwardly upbeat. What we feel inside is not necessarily what we show. Think of the pleasant neighbour who ends up stunning their community when their misdeeds are uncovered. This is not so out of character as we think, but rather a side to them that did not show in their personality. The UK government has had to advise local councils not to name streets after local heroes in case they are one day exposed as far from heroic. Hundreds of streets had to be renamed after the

Jimmy Savile scandal. It was because Lee Harvey Oswald seemed such an unprepossessing individual that most people were convinced he couldn't have acted alone and there must have been a group conspiracy to assassinate President Kennedy.

Personality influences the way we get to where we are going, but it is identity that determines our direction. Identity is more significant in shaping our relationships and how we affect each other. Identity is also more influential in shaping our feel good preferences. In 1950 Erik Erikson, the legendary developmental psychologist, proposed that our identities reflect and define what seems possible for ourselves. Identity matters so much because it primes us to make sense of the world around us and prescribes action. Emotions are our moment by moment guide. Identity is, if you like, our super emotion that guides our long term direction.

If we are asked to describe our personality we would readily have a go. If we were asked to describe our identity we would struggle because identity tends to be nebulous. This need not be the case. Similarly, if asked to describe someone else's personality we wouldn't hesitate. However we would be stumped when it came to their identity. This need not be the case either if we are clearer about the many clues people give away about their identity. Our emotions, attitudes, opinions, beliefs and values all offer insights into our identity.

As discussed earlier, we project ourselves through the personality we show to the world. We also project ourselves through our emotions, attitudes, opinions and so on which reflect our identity. Identity is behind the image we project to others through a myriad of choices, for example, the cars we buy and voluntary good works we do.

We are social beings who have to manage our persona as we navigate our way through our relationships. As we do, we get an idea of how others see us, and so gain some insight into our personality. However, we rarely take up the opportunities we have to discuss our identity. We don't reflect on our identity until life events cause us to think more deeply about ourselves. We are not taught the value of reflecting on our identity. Consequently we are not fully aware of our capacity to construct our identity. The more we understand our identity and the part it plays, and the fact that we can shape it, the more fulfilled we will be. The more coherent our identity, the more able we will be to manage our relationships.

**Identity**

Identity is what defines us, what we like or dislike, what we stand for and identify with. We define ourselves by our physical characteristics, relationships and roles. Our identity evolves as it absorbs our experiences and garners the labels we attach to ourselves. As a result it is constantly being fine-tuned, most actively when we are young, but it continues throughout our life. Lots of small identity adjustments happen all the time and there are also major changes to identity at key transition points in our lives. Rather than think in terms of a single identity it may be more useful to consider that we have multiple layers of identity.

While our draft personality continues to develop throughout childhood, we are born with most of its ingredients in place. However, we only have what we could call 'a starter pack' for our identity. That comes from our family roots, race, gender, nationality and so on. These provide the foundations upon which we build our identity through our life-choices. The sociologist Talcott Parsons, in the 1950s, distinguished between people's 'achieved' and 'ascribed' identities. We have the capacity to consider our identity and determine the extent to which we identify with it. We even have the scope to redefine our ascribed identity, as illustrated in the increasing number of people who want to change their gender. A set of reflection questions are offered in Chapter Eleven to support you to explore your own and other people's identities.

Identity is our prime organiser that gives us our unique perspective on life. No one else sees things quite the same way we do. This is why we:

- warm to others who see the world in a similar way to us

- are wary of anyone who sees it differently

- are so keen to win people round to our own world view

- strongly disapprove of those who grow away from us, especially if they are seen to 'better' themselves.

Why do we have an identity? Bruce Hood, the experimental psychologist, argues that our brain constructs an identity in order to provide a framework upon which we can hang our experiences and give coherence to our lives. We talk about the need to 'gather ourselves together' and to avoid 'falling apart'. Vivian Vignoles, the British social psychologist, believes we form an identity first and foremost in order to feel fulfilled. Our identity also satisfies our need for continuity and lets us believe we remain the same person over time. Our identity thrives as we meet our need to:

- belong (fit in)

- make our lives collectively purposeful (be part of things)

- feel confident we can influence our environments (progress)

- distinguish ourselves from others (make our mark)

It is identity that transforms us. It is our identity, not our personality, that is:

- affected by success and failure

- turned to when we make career choices

- revealed when faced with a significant challenge.

As discussed earlier, personality *disposes* us towards broad areas of aspiration, such as creativity or being active. Identity makes sense of these disposition and *primes* specific personal aspirations. Our dreams and goals emanate principally from our identity. Lack of aspiration is often the result of negative or unformed identities. Kennon Sheldon, the American self-determination theorist, has shown how choosing our aspirations is core to the process of becoming who we want to be. When choosing our aspirations we subconsciously check in with our identity to determine what seems possible. Aspirations and identity work in partnership. Mihaly Csikszentmihalyi in his influential book *Flow: The Psychology of Optimal Experience* concluded that the best moments in our lives come from acting in ways that express who we are.

Our defensive behaviours are always responses to threats to our identity. We don't experience threats to our personality. Defensiveness in all its guises comes either from an inflated, or deflated identity, from feeling superior or inferior to others. When people offend or upset us, we don't fall out with them because they have bruised our personality; what they have bruised is our identity. Their comments jar with and challenge how we see ourselves. We think – 'Do they really think I would do that.' Conversely, the inspiring boss makes their colleagues feel good about themselves and connects them with their positive identity.

Identity has an all-pervading impact on our lives. When we take criticism personally it is our identity that responds. Sexism and racism are particularly toxic because they threaten the aspects of our identity that we didn't choose and can't readily change. More positively, the value of role models is that they prime us to consider possible identities to which 'people like us' can aspire.

A coherent identity will give us confidence and resilience and take us beyond the scope of our personality. It also releases us from needing others' approval or admiration. A coherent identity engenders courage to face challenges. When we aren't sure of who we are or what we stand for challenges become threatening and insurmountable.

Fortunately identity can be readily primed. Whenever we praise an aspect of another person we are priming them to be more aware of that particular aspect of themselves, be it a strength, a passion or an allegiance. When an identity is primed, so also are the emotions and attitudes that go along with that identity.

Helping our children, students and colleagues to construct a positive identity is the greatest service we can offer them. The better we know someone the more readily we can help them shape their identity. If we are respected and liked others will embrace the feedback and advice we give them. Supporting them to make good choices and discover aspirations that excite or interest them will contribute to the growth of their identity. We don't get inspired and start to work on something, we start working on our aspirations and get inspired. Identity primes specific personal aspirations. And we can prime the primer.

We are more likely to persevere with goals which draw upon those aspects of ourselves that are central to our identity. When a challenge fits our identity we think it is worth making the effort to overcome. If not, we see it as 'not for people like us' and give up. The greater clarity we have about our identity and our aspirations, the more likely we are to fulfil our aspirations. One benefit of having a clear passion is that others can more readily proffer support and indeed give gifts that build our passion. In contrast when people don't know our passions, it's hard for them to support us and we get useless gifts! A clear sense of self supports us to pursue realistic aspirations and avoid unrealistic goals. Lack of direction is often due to an under-developed or threatened identity. People who don't know what they want lack the personal compass provided by a clear identity. Successful people know the direction they are growing in.

Daniel Kahneman has found that we are especially motivated to avoid unwanted identities, often more strongly than to pursue desired identities. This is why we clean our house from top to bottom when our mother-in-law is expected. Think of a particular reputation you would dread to have and note the lengths to which you will go to avoid it.

If our identity is constructed from self-perceptions, given what we know about self-deception, does that mean our identity is inevitably flawed? Helpfully, our identity is also gleaned from the perceptions others have of us. This acts as a counterweight to our own subjective perception. Feedback from others shapes, to varying degrees, our identity; an idea Charles Coolley captured at the beginning of the twentieth century in his term 'looking glass self'.

## Social Identity

In addition to *personal identity*, we also have a *social identity*. This is our perception of our 'collective selves', who we are together, 'people like us'. The world famous Bristol-based social psychologist, Henri Tajfel, posited that we invariably identify with and think well of any group we join because we want to think well of ourselves. We tune in immediately to even the most trivial of group identities. Think how quickly we identify with a new group, even for a half hour workshop at a conference.

In our discussion about being part of things we saw how we rein in selfishness because the benefits we can achieve in a group are greater than acting on our own. As well as great benefits, social identity can bring us problems. Claude Steele has shown that feeling devalued on the basis of our group tends to undermine our confidence. What he termed *stereotype threat* is a trip switch within us that triggers an anxiety that we might conform to the stereotype and become the very thing that we fear.

We know that people tend to stereotype us according to our social identity. Stereotype threat interferes with our thinking, worsens performance and exacerbates anxiety in a vicious cycle. Identity threat is diffuse, which means we have to remain vigilant. It preoccupies and takes hold of us. We have a heightened consciousness of those aspects of our identity that are under attack. Also if our belonging is at risk, we will do what we can to maintain it even if our actions have adverse consequences for us.

Social identity threat is one of the biggest factors in under-achievement and underperformance. Any experience where our group isn't valued is particularly damaging to our achievement. Amin Maalouf, the French essayist, posited a central question for our times; why do people commit horrific crimes in the name of identity? He concluded that when people feel their social identity is under siege, they can do unimaginable things. Equally we can harness the power of social identity for good. For example, in trade unions, international unions and fund raising for charities, all of which can effect unimaginable positive change.

**Attitudes**

Our attitudes are like badges that we display to reveal our identity. We show our attitudes through our behaviour, in particular through the choices we make and the opinions we hold. Attitudes make an early impression on others and can provoke strong reactions.

Our *general attitudes* flow to some extent from our personality. For example, if we are open, we tend to show an enquiring attitude; if agreeable, we are more likely to have cooperative attitudes and if conscientious we show hard working attitudes. Our *social attitudes* are picked up mainly from those prevalent within our groups.

By expressing our attitudes we tell others who we are and what we think of the world. We feel affirmed when we have communicated our attitudes, hence the popularity of social media. Attitudes are contagious within groups because our identities are hypersensitive to the attitudes of our peers.

A key issue in our relationships is other people's cost and benefit to us; what others can do for us and what they need from us. The attitudes we form about others are to a large extent based on how much net value they have for us. These interpersonal attitudes are the currency with which we validate one another. We are normally unaware of the impact our attitudes have on others. When we adopt defensive attitudes, we invariably deceive ourselves. As William Boyd, the Scottish author, commented – 'The last thing we discover in life is our effect.'

Our *interpersonal attitudes* are shaped by our identity. These attitudes bolster and protect our identity, like allies that help us to justify ourselves. For example, an arrogant attitude betrays a superior identity and a submissive attitude comes from an inferior sense of self. When someone adopts a disparaging attitude towards us, it is not their attitude that is the problem, it is their identity. The attitude is simply doing its job to buttress the identity. Attitudes are servants to identity. To understand someone's interpersonal attitude, we need to dig deeper into their identity in that particular context. Our interpersonal attitudes are like the price tag we put on ourselves to show how valuable we think we are. These attitudes are windows into someone's identity and key to predicting how they will behave. They are also invaluable in working out how best to respond to them. We use the Ring to explore the range of interpersonal attitudes, each attitude reflecting the balance between our preference for making our mark and being part of things. See Figure 6 below.

It might be surprising to see *humility* portrayed in the most balanced section of the Ring. Dictionaries often describe humility as meekness. Humble is, however, an appropriate term to describe the attitude that comes from an identity that balances fairness to self and others.

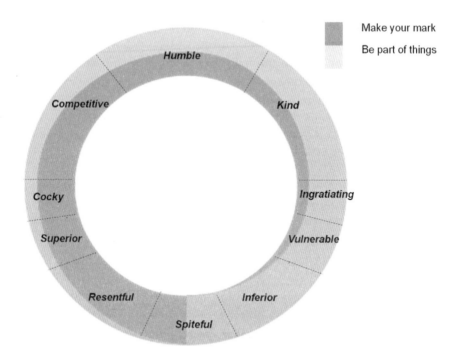

Figure 6 The Ring of Interpersonal Attitudes

Humility is often used somewhat apologetically when, for example, we start a sentence with 'In my humble opinion'. However, people who embody humility are those whom we describe as rounded, grounded or centred. Humility is not the absence of pride, but the capacity to overcome the temptation to feel superior. It is not the absence of selfishness, but the capacity to overcome the temptation to be self-absorbed. Humility doesn't mean stooping to look smaller than we are, but rather standing side by side with something larger than us in a way that brings home our relative smallness. It is feeling good about ourselves and feeling good about others.

Humility is a fruitful attitude in two ways. Firstly it creates an abundance for both ourselves and others by:

- achieving personal priorities while at the same time contributing to a shared purpose

- using our strengths to the benefit of others

- recognising potential in others and creating opportunities for them to contribute

- being competitive but with a grace that avoids damaging relationships

- being receptive to feedback.

Secondly, humility generates compassion for both ourselves and others by:

- forgiving ourselves and others, realising we all make mistakes

- having a high regard for others but not at the expense of our own worth.

Humility is an antidote to the dark emotions and attitudes. It lets all our qualities shine. We can't judge ourselves as humble; only others can do that. But we can consciously aim to balance our perspective with that of others.

We start to judge one another very early in life, in fact by the age of one we are already judging others by how they interact with us. However we vary along a continuum of judgemental to non-judgemental, from critical to less critical. People high in humility are non-judgemental. The more comfortable we are with ourselves, the less we need to define ourselves by judging others. In contrast, highly judgemental individuals are those with an insecure identity that drives them to be hypercritical of others.

Humility is linked to wisdom. It is understanding the limits of one's knowledge, not being afraid of getting things wrong, an openness to new ideas and being willing to expose ourselves to opposing perspectives.

Figure 7 plots the interpersonal attitudes alongside the matching emotional constellations. As we look at the attitudes around the Ring, to the left we see increasing superiority, while to the right there is increasing inferiority. We can see how the attitudes and emotions in each section mutually drive each other.

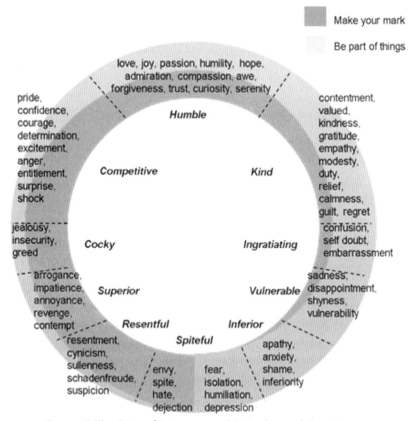

Figure 7 The Ring of Interpersonal Attitudes and Emotions

**Early Identity Development**

In the 1950s Erik Erikson started his pioneering work in the study of identity development. We now know that identity forms over time through our experiences, especially through our emotionally charged experiences which reflect the degree of importance events have for our identity. The thread that holds together all the aspects of our identity and gives continuity to our sense of self is our memory. Identity gets built up through *autobiographical memories* and is constantly being constructed. Erikson's work showed how identity grows through narratives that create our life story and serves to provide us with unity, purpose and meaning. We do this by reconstructing our past, imagining our future and keeping a consistent narrative going. This is why looking back regularly, taking stock and touching base helps us define and refine who we are.

It is thought that the reason we don't remember much as an infant is that we have not yet formed a clear identity within which to hold our memories. By age three, the stories children tell their parents about what has been happening to them help them start to build up their autobiographical memory. Parents who talk with their children regularly about the child's role in family events, their emotions, thoughts and desires help them compile a bank of rich autobiographical memories. Parents can help to mould their children's experiences into meaningful stories that build a strong identity. Young people vividly relish stories where they have been the main character and they never tire of hearing them.

Jane Harter, the self-esteem researcher, contends that infants can't yet globalise their feelings about themselves or value themselves as a whole. However, children, from as early as two years begin to evaluate themselves on specific skills as they become aware of their place in their pecking orders. They experience feelings of positivity or negativity towards particular aspects of themselves and will for example, want to, or not want to, show adults what they have done.

Children begin to discern a clear sense of self around four years of age. At this age it is based on the mainly positive messages their parents and carers communicate to them. Consequently, before eight years of age, most children show uniformly high levels of self-esteem. In addition, their cognitive limitations protect them from thinking too negatively about themselves. Their embryonic perspective-taking capacity means they don't yet have much grasp of what others think of them.

Life changes for children around the age of eight. They now have the cognitive capacity needed to assimilate the evaluations they have been collecting about themselves into a global sense of 'who I am'. They can begin to sum up and value their whole self, 'what I am worth', and develop a fledgling identity. Concern for approval increases sharply, reflected in the emergence of gossip within the peer group.

This is when differences in self-esteem begin to appear, bringing with it a host of emotions like admiration, jealousy and pride. Children around this time start to experience more dark emotions and enjoy fewer bright emotions. They may become more guarded and inhibited. They are starting to grow narrative skills that allow them to integrate their experiences into a life story.

> How selfhood begins with a walking away,
> And love is proved in the letting go.
>
> C. Day-Lewis

During early adolescence there is a shift away from the sense of self which children have formed based on their parents' approval and disapproval, towards their own evaluation of themselves. This is when young people start to claim their own identity.

The identity crisis in adolescence, first identified by Erikson, is marked by an increase in depression rates around 13 years of age. Significantly, a dramatic gender divergence occurs between 15 and 18 with female depression rates double the rate for males. Rates then start to decline post 18 years of age. The hike in depression rates points to the 13 to 18 stage as the second 'pinch point' in identity formation. Identity formation is, in large part, a process of evaluating the self. Young teenagers are acutely sensitive to judgement from others. They experience a heightened self-consciousness, together with a greater susceptibility to peer influence. This explains why adolescents have a tendency to get wrapped up in themselves and show increased risk-taking in the presence of peers.

This chapter has shown how recognising the separate roles of personality and identity can enhance our insight. In particular it has revealed that while we have limited control over our personality we have significant control over our identity, in fact, more control than we might realise. Identity is the most formative part of our development.

The implication of this is significant. Despite the prominence given to personality in our culture, if we want to influence others it is their identity we should fruitfully focus upon. Identity becomes critical in adolescence but this is the culmination of a process that started some years earlier. Most teenagers who have a difficult adolescence will have shown problems earlier in middle childhood. We can help young people make sense of their personality. More importantly we can directly support their sense of self from around the age of four and prime their identity from around eight years of age. This will give them the best start in constructing their identity, a process that will continue throughout their lives.

## CHAPTER EIGHT

# Stances we take

**Until recently, primatologists believed that it was the brain** chemistry of *alpha* primates that enabled them to dominate their groups. But they now know that if an alpha primate is killed another will take over and their testosterone and cortisol levels will rise as a result. Likewise, if a primate gets pushed to the bottom of the group, their hormone profile changes. So brain chemistry is both cause and effect as a primate's position in the group exaggerates any differences. It's the same with humans. Our mental state affects our position in the group, but our position in the group also affects our mental state.

The Ring of Preferences helps us to make sense of and monitor our attitudes, emotions and behaviour as we adapt to social settings. Our inner workings create our *stance*. This is the posture, or attitude, we adopt within our groups and hold on to for a period of time.

Within any group we adopt a stance to help us navigate our way through the group dynamics. The stances framework I have evolved gives us the big picture of how we affect the group and how the group affects us. It provides us with a holistic perspective on group dynamics and a vocabulary to describe our position in the group at any one time. The framework also helps us consider how others relate to the group. Thinking about a colleague's stance provides us with clues as to how we can best respond to them and, of equal importance, what not to do.

Our location on the Ring at any one time represents how we balance being part of things and making our mark. The upper half of the Ring represents successful mixtures of the preferences. On the lower right side the mix is weighted towards being too accommodating – giving way to others at a cost to ourselves. On the lower left side it is weighted towards feeling too entitled – doing our own thing at a cost to others. I have subdivided the Ring into ten stances. These are immediately recognisable and I have used them with children as young as eight. See Figure 8 opposite.

The stances are designed to help us understand people's attitudes and emotions, rather than to pigeonhole or categorise them. The key message is that we can change our stance.

The three stances within the top half of the Ring, *leading*, *performing* and *team playing* are positive and reflect a healthy balance of preferences. The remaining seven stances are defensive – increasingly imbalanced and disconnected. They are disconnected from others on the lower left and disconnected from ourselves on the lower right.

The stances offer a language to reflect upon and discuss our own and others' behaviour and attitude in an impersonal and nonthreatening way. The framework helps us consider more objectively how our own and others' choices affect the group. Taking responsibility is essentially about making choices with an eye to how they impact on others. Let's consider each stance in turn, looking at positive stances first:

■ **Team playing** – In this stance people generally strive to be part of things, and to enjoy low arousal emotions

**Leading** 'go-to' person, respected, sticks up for everyone, shares their knowledge, pulls the group together

**Team Playing** calm, keen to please, dependable, compassionate, cooperative, kind, looks for shared purpose, easy going, observant, modest, avoids attention

**Performing** keen to impress, proud, confident, ambitious, takes risks, speaks out, likes excitement and challenge, shows initiative, faces their fear, can be impatient and insensitive

**People pleasing** needs to please, trouble minding own business, too open, confused, too kind

**Attention seeking** class clown, always trying to be funny, needs to impress, presumptuous

**Taking-things-to-heart** worried about not being liked, vulnerable to being used, over-sensitive, too trusting, puts self down

**Taking-over** arrogant, bossy, agitated, expects special privileges, doesn't care what others think, enjoys annoying authority, feels picked on, reckless, calculating

**Sulking** resentful for being overlooked, imposes their mood on group, not interested in fitting in

**Upset and Angry** stuck, feels powerless, moody, envious, hateful, holds grudges, spiteful, feels humiliated, given up, can't control emotions

**Hiding** shy, easily embarrassed, fearful of making mistakes, hides feelings

Figure 8 The Stances

like contentedness and kindness. This means they have a calming and steadying effect on others. In this stance individuals are happy to be in the shadow of limelight-seeking people and don't feel the need to put themselves forward. Their drive is to value others and contribute to the shared purpose.

■ **Performing** – People adopting this stance are keen to make their mark and they participate with a competitive edge. They seek out opportunities to display their individuality and enjoy high arousal emotions such as pride and excitement. These help keep them motivated for action. They may find it hard to accommodate the other group members and can be impatient with some colleagues.

■ **Leading** – In the leading stance individuals manage to achieve a balance between their own and others' needs. They see the big picture and know intuitively how to make everyone feel involved and get the best from them. People become leaders when they can balance their confidence with humility and self-deprecating humour. They can also temper their passion and drive with a sense of fun. In time they come to epitomise the group and make the group matter.

■ **People-pleasing** – This stance reflects people's self-doubt and confusion or over-awareness of others' needs. They believe the safest approach is to try to be agreeable to everyone and their self-doubt can push them to being overly kind. Folk adopting this stance have unclear personal goals and prefer to be directed and led by others.

■ **Taking-things-to-heart** – This stance is driven by vulnerability and self-blame that leads to a submissive attitude. In some respects it can be seen as a cry for help. In this stance people's sense of self-worth is slender making them open to being exploited by others. They are easily upset by others and internalise the hurt. They think they have no right to make a fuss.

■ **Hiding** – This stance is all about protecting the private, internal self and this drive consequently outweighs any desire for self-enhancement or attention. People who adopt this stance hurt in private, so they don't hurt others. They feel inferior and dread making a fool of themselves in front of peers and so try to hide their anxiety. People hide when they have low self-belief or low status, or when they experience a situation as unpredictable and out of their control. They believe that it is safer to opt out rather than risk failure.

■ **Attention-seeking** – The attention-seeking stance emerges from a 'me-me-me' sense of entitlement. There is invariably a status insecurity or a false confidence that is driving their desperation to impress. They can't get the status they want legitimately and so make themselves stand out in unproductive, diversionary and exasperating ways.

■ **Taking-over** – This stance reflects a selfish, superior and dominating attitude that is shown in oppositional and calculating behaviour. People in this stance don't try to persuade or explain, they just demand and antagonise. Their lack of empathy combined with their sense of entitlement means they are happy to alienate and demean others.

■ **Sulking** – People take the sulking stance when they expect special treatment but don't get it. They then feel overlooked and become resentful. In a passive aggressive, but highly visible, way they make sure everyone knows how bad they are feeling.

■ **Upset and angry** – There are two ways people can fall into this stance. In one way individuals focus on what is wrong with them, dwell on their negative emotions and are unable to self-soothe. In the other way individuals show bad tempered mood swings that leave them prone to hostility towards others. Either way, the result is a desperate attempt to regain control and to try to hold the self together. Both approaches are invariably self-defeating.

The stances, as psychological states, are not so much good or bad as useful or not useful in any given situation. To be a well-rounded and resilient person it is necessary to experience most of, if not all of, the stances. There will be situations when each of the stances is appropriate. For example, it makes sense to *hide* initially in staff meetings with a new boss! It can be useful for the group to have people who want to *take over* as, among other things, they are able to face uncertainty without fear. Some oppositional behaviour helps insulate us against groupthink. Innovators need to be willing to take risks, to challenge convention and do things others might disapprove of. Adopting the *upset and angry* stance and giving voice to our distress can bring relief and attract support.

However, it is not constructive to get stuck in any of the defensive stances. This can happen when we form habits and the associated emotions endure and become absorbed into our identity. People's anger, grievance, self-doubt or vulnerability can become part of their sense of self.

The defensive stances are related to strong dark emotions but, if we can reflect on what makes these emotions happen and what they make us do, they can help us learn from experience and become more psychologically mature.

We can use the stances to reflect on what we need to do to rebalance ourselves in any context. The framework allows us to be aware of the stance we adopt and what causes this. It helps us to figure out what gets us into a particular stance on a bad day, and the best thing we can do to work our way out of this stance and back into our typical 'good day' stance.

For example, if we catch ourselves in the attention-seeking stance, is it because we like the sound of our own voice? What would be a more useful way to get the status we are looking for? If we find ourselves spending too much time in hiding, what is it about ourselves and the context we are in that encourages us to adopt this stance? Are we out of the loop, are we unprepared, are we being ignored? Can we identify what we can contribute to the group, or do we need to get out of this situation altogether? If we find ourselves sulking, we need to ask 'what is this achieving?' What do we want to achieve and what positive stance might be better?

We shouldn't take our positive stances for granted. When we have effectively chaired a meeting we can pause to reflect on how our behaviour made such a positive impact, how we kept the group to time, how we ensured every voice was heard and how we achieved a consensus. We can identify our signature strengths when we reflect on our time as a team player – how we use banter to maintain the shared purpose, how we challenge colleagues not just support them. If our natural good day stance is performing, how are we achieving our own agenda without being seen as self-centred and dismissive of others? How are we making the most of our talents and confidence while earning the respect of our colleagues?

Thinking about how best to respond to other people's feel-good preferences gives us important clues. Broadly speaking –

■ people whose priority is to be liked and valued will respond best to an approach focused on common purpose and team work

■ people who prioritise control and personal success will appreciate opportunities to forge ahead and attain status and will be energised by an audience and competition

■ personal affirmation is a useful approach to take with individuals showing a submissive and inferior attitude

■ explicit negotiation is an appropriate strategy with individuals displaying a superior and arrogant attitude.

At the same time it is important to encourage assertive individuals to appreciate the benefits of sharing and to help the more accommodating to take the initiative occasionally.

The stances are a window into our own and others' emotions, attitudes and identities, while at the same time providing an external framework that allows us to reflect on ourselves and others in an impartial and non-emotive way. As Ben White, a teacher colleague, said, 'I am really taken with the way in which the stances help bring measured analysis into a context which is often filled with emotive judgements, moralizing or exasperation.'

**Personalising our response**

We can use the following information on the stances to choose the best response for individuals and avoid the worst response. This is summarised in the table below.

**Leading**

The optimal response to adopt for individuals in this stance is a *facilitating* response. For example, give them exclusive responsibility for planning and executing projects. We should be careful not to over-rely on them or hold them up as favourites.

**Performing**

Here the priority is to give them the opportunity to challenge themselves and access status. This calls for a *directive* response but one that gives them high profile responsibilities that optimise their organisational skills. The worst thing we can do is to suppress their initiative with oppressive regulations.

**Team Playing**

The key is to create opportunities that draw team players into the common purpose through an *inviting* response. For example, provide them with purposeful responsibilities within the team. Least helpful responses trigger their vulnerability to turn in on themselves by being intrusive or making a fuss of them.

| Overview of Stances | | | | |
| --- | --- | --- | --- | --- |
| **Stance** | **Attitude** | **Preference** | **Best response** | **Worst response** |
| Leading | Humble | Get best from self and group | Facilitating | Holding them up as stars |
| Performing | Competitive | Promote self to achieve status | Directing | Suppressing |
| Team playing | Kind | Seek shared purpose to be valued | Inviting | Intruding |
| Attention-seeking | Cocky | Be noticed | Limit setting | Over-stimulating |
| People-pleasing | Ingratiating | Be liked | Reaffirming at all costs | Over-taxing with responsibilities |
| Taking-over | Superior | Do own thing, at cost to others | Negotiating | Retaliating |
| Taking-things-to-heart | Inferior | Put self down, to seek reassurance | Unconditionally accepting | Colluding |
| Sulking | Resentful | Seek revenge | Constructivley critical | Ignoring |
| Hiding | Fearful | Keep attention off self | Coaxing | Exposing |
| Upset and angry | Spiteful | Spoil things for everyone | Soothing | Pitying |

**Attention-seeking**

A *limit setting* response provides proactive attention and certainty of boundaries. For example, minimise choices and set clearly achievable goals. The worst response is, for example, distracting them by, highlighting comparisons between them and more successful peers.

**People-Pleasing**

The most useful approach is a *reaffirming* response. For example, remind them of the common purpose and the value of their contribution or help them make choices for themselves.

We cannot afford to add to their self-doubt and so need to avoid showing dislike or exasperation.

**Taking-over**

The aim has to be to let them express their individuality through a *negotiating* response. For example, seek advice from them and so offer the prestige they crave. This invites them to make a commitment to become part of the solution. It's important not to exacerbate their grievance by reacting with harsh criticism or public ridicule.

**Taking-things-to-heart**

For people who feel anxious and vulnerable, how others perceive them is crucial. We instinctively react to vulnerable people with pity. Asking why they're upset doesn't help as it is likely to trigger rumination. It is better to help them to step back and visualise their experience as if they are a fly on the wall. This counteracts their typical self-immersion. This lets them reappraise events in a more thoughtful and less emotional way. An *unconditionally accepting* response will help them replace harsh self-judgments with self-acceptance. For example, communicate that we are there for them because we want to be, not because we have to be, support them to set their own goals and ambitions, or help them by supporting a cause that is important to them. Helping them to focus on values that transcend themselves is better than focusing on any particular threat.

**Sulking**

The most effective *constructively criticising* response includes giving them opportunities to rebuild a sense of status. We need to give them a reality check with clear feedback on their unreasonable behaviour. 'I'd like to challenge the attitude I'm picking up' is better than saying – 'I don't like your attitude.' The worst reaction is to treat them with indifference and ignore them. This is their biggest fear and can make them feel paranoid as they assume the lack of feedback means that we are hostile to them.

## Hiding

People who are worried about being rejected brood about what others think of them. We need to build their confidence through a persistent but sensitive *coaxing* response. For example, give advance notice to help them contribute to discussions, highlight their strengths and build on these in ways that can benefit others. We often assume that the best way to help people cope with performance anxiety is to help them calm down. However, research has shown that reframing anxiety as excitement and saying aloud 'I am excited', leads to an opportunity, as opposed to a threat, mindset. The worst response is to expose their vulnerabilities by putting them on the spot or under time pressure, or leaving them unsure as to what will happen next.

## Upset and angry

We need to restore some level of self-acceptance through opportunities to experience positive emotions. Engineering moments for them to manifest personal adequacy can provide a psychological foothold. We need to offer a *soothing* response. For example, use planning time to emphasise predictability, acknowledge their distress, mirror and contextualise their confusion and give shape to their perplexing emotions. Least helpful responses include making too many demands or pitying them.

CHAPTER NINE
# Styles of influence

**Think of all the bosses you have ever had. Now try sorting them** by the way they made you feel. What you are contemplating is their leadership style. Any individual with authority and responsibility for others relates to them through their *style*.

How do you think people would describe you? Cold and distant? Scary? Friendly and enthusiastic? Someone who inspires respect? A bit of a pushover? A good laugh but not someone to take seriously?

It is our style that determines our effectiveness as leaders, parents or teachers. And this is in large part down to how we affect others. Our style mediates in part our authority and, in particular, how much autonomy we support in others.

If we have responsibility for others we need to build relationships that balance support and challenge. We do this through what I like to call the four WISE principles: Warmth, Independence, Sharing-the-reins and Encouragement. The table below illustrates how these principles help us to meet the psychological needs of those we are responsible for.

| Principle | Others' need for |
|---|---|
| **W**armth | Fitting in, to seek acceptance |
| **I**ndependence | Making our mark, to achieve status |
| **S**haring the reins | Being part of things, to feel valued |
| **E**ncouragement | Making progress, to achieve |

Two of the principles relate to support and two to challenge:

**SUPPORT**

**Warmth**

We are approachable and create a climate where people feel they can be themselves.

**Sharing-the-reins**

We maximise a sense of common purpose, through partnership, fun, humour and banter. We show curiosity about people's interests, aspirations and opinions and are open to being influenced by them. We invite their contribution as a valued partner.

**CHALLENGE**

**Encouragement**

Encouragement comes from personalised, achievable and specific goals. It inspires people's curiosity and fires their enthusiasm. When we encourage we help individuals to recognise their strengths and areas for growth. We make them feel responsible for their progress. We give them a vision of who they can become. Encouragement is literally putting courage into the other person to stretch themselves.

**Independence**

We create a structure that clarifies accountability. We give opportunities for choices, decision-making, exercising responsibility, risk taking and learning from mistakes. Independence can also involve criticism and demand for more effort.

Here's a small exercise I'd like you to do. Thinking of your relationships with those for whom you have responsibility, distribute 20 points between support and challenge. For example, you might give 12 to support and 8 to challenge. Now multiply your two numbers, for example 8X12= 96. Make a note of your score now and I'll explain what it means soon.

As leaders, parents and teachers we are never in neutral. We are either energising or draining our colleagues, children or students, benefiting or hindering them, validating or invalidating them.

Providing warmth and sharing the reins give the nutrients of support for people's positive emotions and identities. Through warm, non-judgmental relationships we show that we care about others and want to get to know them as individuals. Support helps us connect with others' aspirations, interests and concerns. Because belonging is our deepest need, support is an essential precursor to challenge. The quality of our support will determine how receptive others are to our challenge.

But without the stretch provided by challenge support risks becoming a form of over-protection. Offering encouragement and fostering independence create challenge. Challenge offers the catalyst for people's positive emotions and extends their identities. It starts with an authoritative structure that sets limits but allows people to express their individuality and stretches them to maximise their talents. It stems from achievable goals and information that lets colleagues know how they are progressing. Challenge helps individuals to recognise their achievements, strengths and potential. However, without the balance provided by support, challenge can be threatening. This brings us back to the need for balance between support and challenge.

The Spirals of Support and Challenge can be used to aid reflection on our styles and to enable a dialogue with others about the balance of support and challenge we provide. See Figure 9 below.

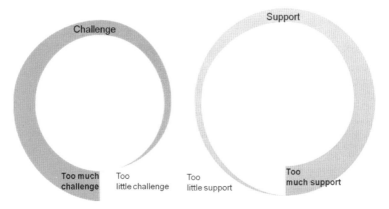

Figure 9 The Spirals of Support and Challenge

If support and challenge were mutually exclusive we could add their affect together to get their cumulative impact. But they are not mutually exclusive. Because the two forces impinge on each other, the *beneficence* of our leadership, parenting and teaching equates to support *multiplied* by challenge. We can't make up for deficiencies in one by maximising the other. We need both support and challenge in balance, one moderating the other. Being low on one approach actually undermines the other. Too much challenge with too little support creates an over-demanding coercion, causing psychological threat. Too much support combined with insufficient challenge forms an under-demanding collusion, leading to apathy.

Figure 10 presents support and challenge as complementary forces. Any mix within the upper half of the Ring is healthy and adaptive. The lower half illustrates how the mix has become imbalanced in one of two directions, either towards being over-demanding or over-protective.

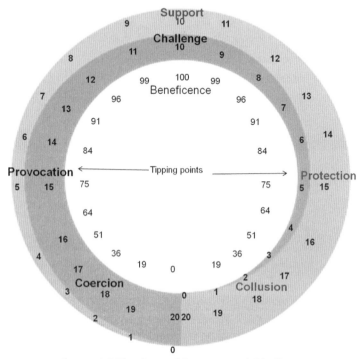

Figure 10 The Ring of Support and Challenge

The paired numbers on the spirals always add up to 20, but their product (inside the Ring) will vary from 0 to 100, reflecting the compound impact of support and challenge. The proud team leader who rated herself or himself as 17 on the challenge spiral needs to realise that the quality of their impact is likely to be reduced when they rate their support as 3. (17 X 3=51)

I have designed my free, online *Leader, Inspire Ring* and

*Parent* profiles to help us as leaders, teachers and parents, to reflect on how we balance support and challenge. This Ring is sub-divided into sections which represent the styles, as you can see in Figure 11 below.

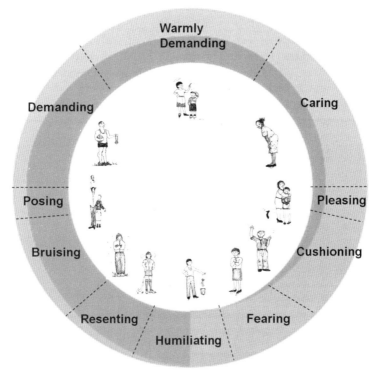

Figure 11 The Styles

Three styles are positive and seven are defensive. I have given them labels that represent the prominent characteristic of each style, remembering that we will almost certainly move between these depending on circumstances, not least how we're feeling on any given day. The style framework is designed to help us reflect not only on our strengths but also on our defensive styles when we are operating below par. Below I set out the relevance of these styles to team leaders.

## The Positive styles

### ■ Demanding

This pushy style prioritises challenge over support. 'Go for it' leaders take a directive approach and are pacesetters who lead by example, getting as much work done, as quickly as possible. They are goal orientated and set high standards and expectations. Their enthusiasm and drive for success is infectious. As they give priority to progress they may be reluctant to make allowances for individual vulnerabilities.

### ■ Caring

This warm style prioritises support over challenge, making colleagues feel accepted and comfortable. They take an invitational approach and are wary of putting pressure on colleagues. Caring leaders are kind, approachable and reassuring and relate to colleagues in a calm and patient manner. There is a danger that they give priority to people's needs over purpose.

### ■ Warmly demanding

Many qualities are common to both the demanding and caring styles, including being focused, helpful, even-handed and respectful. These qualities are also seen in the *warmly demanding* style. This style optimally blends both support and challenge, reflecting the leader's humility and ability to adapt flexibly to get it right for each individual and ensure efficiency. Improvisation is not just 'winging it', there is order to their improvisation. They are tight on standards but know when to exert pressure and when to ease off. With their pitch perfect mix of authority and diplomacy they have the capacity to reprimand people without belittling them. The warmth of their support sets the foundation that allows them to challenge colleagues in a way that builds a sense of corporate pride

**The Defensive Styles**

Just as there are energising mixes of support and challenge, there are also threatening or inhibiting combinations. For example, the demanding style is effective as long as it is accompanied by warmth, but as soon as it is combined with toxins such as judgemental criticism, indifference or arrogance, the leader may be respected but feared or even hated. Similarly a caring style is effective only if the leader is efficient and knowledgeable. Caring without competence will be seen as weak.

If our style becomes too one-sided, it leaves us with little room to manoeuvre and it doesn't take much to push us into a defensive style. We adopt defensive styles when we feel threatened, or when our own needs crowd out our capacity to respond to the needs of colleagues. I have called these defensive styles – *Pleasing, Cushioning, Fearing, Posing, Bruising, Resenting* and *Humiliating*.

■ **Pleasing**
This style tries to accommodate everyone's needs but the slow progress frustrates colleagues. These leaders' attention is easily diverted. Their self-doubt can make them indecisive and hard to take seriously and they struggle to assert their authority. Their pleasing style promises a lot but often fails to deliver. They try to help too much, like an over-attentive waiter or a 'helicopter parent'.

■ **Cushioning**
The cushioning leader may fail to set clear goals and boundaries, be laissez-faire in their approach, let

colleagues be over familiar, or sidestep challenging feedback. This saccharine style gives unmerited praise and tries to protect colleagues and so creates dependency or apathy. Their own vulnerability is contagious and undermines the collective sense of security or cohesion.

### ■ Fearing

With this style the leader is fearful of challenging colleagues. This undemanding style is inhibiting. Such a pedestrian style communicates a lack of direction, ambition and confidence. They give little feedback and their low commitment rubs off on colleagues who, in turn, fail to produce their best work because nobody will appreciate it anyway!

### ■ Posing

In this mode the leader is driven by a mix of ambition and insecurity and their priority is to display his or her expertise rather than develop their colleagues. They use colleagues as an audience to impress. Their keenness to show off can pre-empt any real partnership and leads to superficial relationships. Posing leaders tend to be egocentric, talk too much, in particular about themselves, and are quick to credit themselves for any success. They may try to be funny but their miscued humour has the opposite effect.

### ■ Bruising

The most prominent characteristic of the bruising leader is being overly provocative and insensitive. Leaders can get away with being demanding so long as their colleagues respect and trust them. The demanding style can segue into a highly conditional 'get it right, or else' style. Leaders who are overly focused on what they can 'get out of' their colleagues are blinded to how they affect them and their 'just-get-it-done' mentality rides roughshod over other people.

■ **Resenting**

When leaders come across as resentful they give the impression that they dislike colleagues. This style is high on disdain and low on warmth. Such leaders communicate as little as possible and when they do, they can come across as begrudging or sarcastic. They communicate pomposity through their lack of humour. Judgemental fault-finding dominates their feedback, as they focus on what's wrong and withhold praise. Colleagues have to prove their worth. They are approving only as long as colleagues meet their expectations. They are also prone to favouritism. Resenting leaders play people off against each other in order to weaken opposition. They make colleagues dependent on them but in the process undermine group harmony.

■ **Humiliating**

This style emerges in one of two ways, either through the self-loathing cushioning/fearing route or the colleague-loathing bruising/resenting route. Consider the cushioning leader who allows others to go too far until eventually the leader's patience snaps. Their style may not only smother colleagues but also their own emotions and this can leave them with unexpressed anger that eventually comes out in uncontrolled rage. Alternatively this style can occur in a more calculated way, when leaders stop caring about the people they are responsible for. They ridicule a colleague to 'encourage' others. If sustained for any length of time this style leads to organisational and personal crises.

We can use the Ring once again to gain insight into the emotions and attitudes that shape the styles, as displayed in Figure 12 below.

We can probably relate to elements of all of the styles from

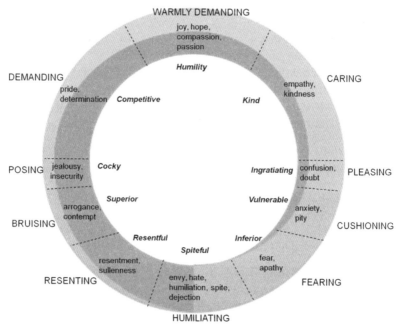

Figure 12 Styles, Emotions and Attitudes

our own experience of leaders. A more challenging question is whether we see ourselves in some of them? Different colleagues need a different approach. Some need to be pushed, others need a metaphorical hug. It is most productive if we try to operate within the positive styles but have the ability to forgive ourselves and move on when we have lapsed into the defensive styles. The more we are aware of our default good day style and its strengths as well as the bad day style we might adopt when stressed or threatened, the better placed we are to give the best of ourselves and get the best from others.

## CHAPTER TEN

# Collective ambition

**Every organisation has its unique culture – the climate we** experience the moment we walk through its doors. Culture influences what happens, who fits in and who doesn't, and what it feels like to be part of that establishment. Organisational culture is an evolving, shared exchange within which colleagues agree values, standards, ideas and information. It is a kind of *collective affect* that can be felt, like the tone of a meeting; it radiates mood. Organisational culture also absorbs and reflects staff morale and stress levels. It influences attitudes which, in turn, shape the culture in a series of reciprocal processes.

So culture shapes behaviour, which shapes culture; culture shapes individual well-being which in turn shapes culture. Culture is also a form of collective identity, an invisible organising force. As such, it is a powerful lever. Well-being is not simply the preserve of the individual for it emerges from the balanced satisfaction of personal, organisational and communal needs. Well-being is something we generate together in a way that creates culture. In this sense culture is a form of collective well-being.

When we describe an organisation's culture we are subjectively summing up how we feel about the organisation. We become more aware of a culture when we go into a new institution, or when different cultures merge, or when something goes well or badly. We feel the force of a culture most strongly when we try to change it or act against it.

Edgar Schein, the American management professor, describes the twin challenges organisations face in adapting to their environment and becoming integrated. It is this integration which is the essence of culture. In a similar way to identity, a culture generates attitudes to bolster itself and thus maintain its integrity.

Although no one person can control a culture, Schein believes it emanates chiefly from the beliefs and attitudes of leaders. Leaders create the culture through the attitudes they show towards colleagues; the staff they appoint; the way they delegate tasks; the information they disseminate; and the resources they make available. What leaders consistently pay attention to powerfully communicates their values. Making their expectations explicit is the most effective strategy for leaders to create a healthy culture. This is because people much prefer structure and consistency to uncertainty. Leaders who blow hot and cold create anxiety and agitation throughout the organisation.

Culture comes mainly from the top but it is constantly re-enacted through everyone's attitudes. Culture is perpetuated through the stories that are shared, particularly legendary stories that explain 'how we got here'. It comes from shared emotional experiences of success and failure. Especially influential are people's emotional responses to crises and how they handle them. Negative attitudes spread insidiously but, thankfully, positive attitudes are equally infectious.

As well as a corporate culture most organisations also have a set of subcultures. Working out the criteria for who is included and who is excluded from the different subcultures is a good way to find out about the culture. A key challenge for leaders is to ensure that the subcultures are aligned as much as possible with the corporate culture.

Culture operates on three dimensions –

1. What people do

2. What people say

3. What people think and feel.

Within healthy cultures all three dimensions are in harmony. In unhealthy cultures there is inconsistency between the dimensions that creates organisational confusion and floundering both of which generate collective and individual stress.

A well-integrated culture draws individuals together through shared purpose and commitment. It creates a strong alignment of values, beliefs, attitudes and behaviour. However, culture doesn't always exert a uniform effect. Individuals don't passively absorb culture, rather they actively engage with it. Organisational culture constructs identities for the staff as a group but also, in part, for individuals. For some their personal identity will be validating, for others it can be undermining.

People's individual needs are fulfilled in varying degrees by the culture, which in turn is then reflected in their commitment to the organisation. However, the major challenge to leaders is to create a culture where divergent views are welcomed and any ensuing tension is channelled creatively. In a healthy culture the impact of frustration and cynicism is aired and so defused by an open leadership style in which everyone's contribution is respected and all views are listened to. Negative attitudes usually have some foundation, although the dark emotions driving them can be so strong as to blind people to positive aspects of the organisation. However by listening carefully to critical comments and acting to address the issues raised, or taking the trouble to explain what lies behind unpopular decisions, leaders can minimise frustration and cynicism.

Amy Edmondson in a landmark study of organisational culture coined the term 'psychological safety' to describe cultures where it is safe to ask for help, admit mistakes or raise tough issues. Most important to psychological safety in any culture is mutual respect which enables a collective willingness to show vulnerability. In such a culture expressions of vulnerability can further deepen shared respect.

Leaders strive for consistency across the staff team. However, rather than seek uniformity, a more realistic aspiration is to strive for healthy cohesion within a framework of shared standards. This allows colleagues to express their individuality through a diversity of practice, but within a unity of purpose.

Cultures are shaped by the way leaders balance challenge and support, as well as by the way individuals balance their feel good preferences for making their mark and being part of things.

The four WISE principles can help us to consider the health of a particular culture.

**Support**

**Warmth**

- How welcoming the atmosphere

- The way people treat one another

- The collective sense of belonging

**Sharing the reins**

- The way we do things

- A shared understanding of common purpose

- How communication flows through the organisation

**Challenge**

**Encouragement**

- What people get recognition for

- The degree to which innovation and creativity are encouraged

- How people are supported towards improvement and advancement

**Independence**

- Delegation

- Leadership opportunities

- Transparency of pecking orders and promotions

In Figure 13 below, I have used the Spirals of support and challenge to chart the key characteristics of different cultures in geographical climate terms. I have depicted the main emotions in capitals whilst showing the main interpersonal attitudes for each culture in italics.

Challenging leaders, along with individuals with a preference for making their mark, create the grease that drives improvement, innovation and change. Demanding leaders and ambitious individuals generate an infectious pressure that drives everyone. However, if challenge and making our mark dominate a culture,

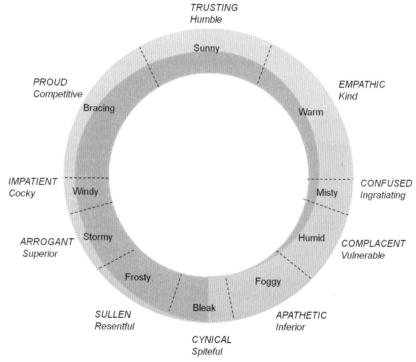

Figure 13 Organisational Cultures

inequality, conflict and favouritism are likely to undermine trust. Too many people are busy building their own empires. Challenge and making our mark, with their inherent individual goals, don't prioritise affiliation, and in fact they can undermine it. People fail to appreciate the contribution made by each individual. In such cultures only a few can thrive.

Equality and fairness are core values in a healthy culture. They are pre-conditions for harmony. Support, together with a preference for being part of things, provides the glue which helps create a unified culture. The ensuing solidarity in turn empowers, but also holds in check, making our mark and prevents people pulling in different directions. This cohesion maximises achievement and innovation. It can't happen the other way round.

It's undeniable that people who trust one another cooperate better. Trusting cultures create collegiality. A flourishing culture capitalises on the positive identities and emotions that flow from personal and collective progress. Colleagues need to be mutually supportive before they can challenge one another. They earn the right to challenge by being trustworthy and committed to the same goals. Collegiality makes it possible for everyone, individually and collectively, to achieve more. Support and challenge, being part of things and making our mark create a culture which aligns with what organisational experts Doug Ready and Emily Truelove call 'collective ambition'.

CHAPTER ELEVEN
# Growing insight

**Hopefully you have had some 'light bulb' moments as we** have worked through the Ring and its different applications. I have had lots working on this book. I am particularly keen for readers to develop insight, greater objectivity and honest self-reflection. For me personal insight is understanding ourselves within our relationships and knowing how others see us. A nine-year-old girl captured it neatly in a workshop when I asked what she found useful about the profiles I had developed. She wrote 'the profile made me reflect on things about me I hadn't known before.'

Insight comes from self-reflection. Peter Drucker, the founder of modern management, extols the virtue of reflection: 'Follow effective action with quiet reflection. From the quiet reflection, will come even more effective action.' We also know from research that people who possess deeper self-insight enjoy stronger relationships and greater well-being.

For centuries philosophers have believed that introspection is a virtuous activity. However, introspection is not insight. Thinking about ourselves doesn't necessarily lead to knowing ourselves. Insight is qualitatively different from introspection. In fact, Anthony Grant, the Australian coaching psychologist, has found that introspection alone can actually make things worse and damage our well-being.

Tasha Eurich, the American organisational psychologist, points out some of the common pitfalls of introspection. She believes we mislead ourselves when we think that the answer to our problems lies deep within us and that introspection will uncover it. We search for a definitive 'truth' to figure ourselves out. This blinds us to the nuances of life. If an adult with a particular relationship problem continually asks themselves 'why', all that results is the stirring up of negative emotions. Eurich says that whenever we ask why, we are usually seeking a single, unequivocal answer to what is invariably a complex question. Once we have come up with an answer we assume it's correct and stop being curious. We rationalise things to justify ourselves. The danger is that we end up being more confused and trapped in the past.

Insight is essentially solution-focused, allowing us to find out *what* we can learn. Instead of puzzling over *why* we are the kind of person we are, it is better to ask – *what* kind of person are we? Asking what, keeps us curious about ourselves. When dealing with emotional problems it is more productive to ask 'what is happening?' and 'what am I feeling?' This encourages us to name the emotion and this helps us stay in control. Rather than ask 'why do you want to change your job?', it is better to ask 'what do you dislike about your current job? *Why* questions draw us to our limitations and barriers. But *what* questions open up our thinking about our potential.

Rumination, a form of anxious introspection, is a major, and common, barrier to insight. It's often triggered when we feel we don't measure up in areas that are important to us and then we experience guilt or shame. Rumination is dwelling on problems in a way that generates more negative predictions. The subsequent self-reproaching emotions make us resistant to feedback and create further barriers to insight.

One of the things that perpetuates rumination for some people is the belief that worry is a good thing, that it can help prepare us for bad outcomes and solve problems. Some people can't stop worrying until they've solved every problem. For them negative moods translate into more worrying.

We can take action to combat a low mood such as going for regular walks as walking acts as a powerful mood lifter. Humans evolved to search for food and other rewards and, as a result, positive emotions are linked with moving. Allocating a specific time slot for worrying can help limit the extent of our worrying. To keep perspective on an issue we can ask ourselves 'does anyone else really care about this?' Most people don't actually bother about our flaws as much as we do. Another option is to distract ourselves. The best distractions are those with a fast reward, like cleaning windows, seeing friends or exercise.

Self-reflection is a means to an end, and to intentional change. It's not an easy process as it can generate feelings of agitation, vulnerability and defensiveness, but nonetheless it leads to valuable insights.

**Tips for developing insight**

- Grow a mindset of curiosity.

- Ask what rather than why.

- Imagine yourself from another person's vantage point.

- Scrutinise your errors, they may reveal your subconscious thinking.

- Notice when you find yourself laughing at yourself. As George Bernard Shaw mused, 'When a thing is funny, search it carefully for a hidden truth'.

- Calmly consider evidence that challenges your beliefs.

■ Take personal responsibility and avoid blaming others.

■ Set yourself challenging questions. For example, how might you be contributing to your least enjoyable relationship at work? How might you help to change this?

■ Schedule reflection time and commit to it.

■ Start small. If half an hour of reflection seems too much, try ten minutes.

■ Work with a colleague on joint reflection to help you commit.

■ Consciously stop and reflect on what emotions you felt during a particular period.

■ Cultivate the experience of awe, to get distance and perspective.

There are a variety of ways we can develop insight through committing our thoughts to paper. Expressive writing is only of benefit if we include both the factual and emotional aspects of events. Insight comes from the powerful combination of thoughts and emotions. I outline some of these writing exercises below.

**Predicting**

We can check out the assumptions we make about ourselves, and the world, by recording our predictions of what is going to happen with what actually does happen, especially when we make big decisions. The psychologist Gary Klein suggests doing a 'pre-mortem'. Imagine you are one year into the future. You have implemented the plan you have just drawn up and the outcome was a disaster. Write a short history of that disaster. This process will reveal potential pitfalls.

**Self-affirmation**

This is a process of writing about our core values. It involves writing a brief essay about what is important to us, how and why these things are important and when they have been important. This process can bring about a more expansive view of our self. It taps into our valued identity and helps us gain perspective on what really matters. Self-affirmation is a particularly useful way to cope with identity threat because it puts any threat in the context of the big picture. Self-affirmation is most useful in coping with critical feedback if it's completed before receiving the feedback.

**Daily review**

This requires that we review what went well today and what didn't go well? What did we learn? What can we do better?

**Processing trauma**

James Pennebaker, the pioneer of writing therapy, has found a remarkably effective way of processing trauma. This involves writing for fifteen minutes each day for four days about our deepest thoughts and feelings, regarding what happened to us and how it affected our lives. The only rule is that once you begin writing, continue to do so until your time is up. This process works by developing a narrative that helps us make sense of our experiences.

**Being solution focused**

The 'miracle question' is a simple but powerful tool from Solution Focused Brief Therapy, developed by Steve de Shazer in the 1980s. Imagine that during the night a miracle happens and your issue has been solved and your life has greatly improved. How is your life going to be different? What is the first thing you notice in the morning that has changed? This gives us a picture of our desired future and primes us to notice specific improvements. It helps us think more broadly about our aspirations.

**Being mindful**

Awareness has been described as our 'meta perception'. Awareness makes use of both thinking and emotions, but is larger than our thoughts and emotions. Our sense of self partly emerges from our emotions and thoughts, but it is also apart from them. Jon Kabat-Zinn argues convincingly that awareness is like a melting pot, which integrates everything about the individual. He and others have made accessible the rich resource of mindfulness. Mindfulness is imagining ourselves from a high vantage point of awareness that trumps both thinking and emoting, to let us acknowledge our passing thoughts and emotions. Mindfulness, as defined by Ellen Langer, a famous 1970s Harvard psychologist, is the process of seeing ourselves and the world differently, and then acting on these observations. Most people consider mindfulness to mean simply meditating, but it involves more than that. It is enhanced by getting outdoors running, hiking, cycling, horse riding or walking, indeed any activity that gives us head space to help us stay focused in the present.

Generally, we need to select a reflection process that suits us. No one can tell us how to do it. We need to capture our thinking and log our insights to help us sustain any change. We need to dig deep to explore the processes underlying our behaviour. Many people reflect through writing in a journal. Talking with someone we trust may be more suitable. Self-reflection requires some form of external sounding board or mirror that helps us to stand back and gain perspective. Use the Ring below to consider which aspects of your main goal makes you feel. . .

Figure 14 Which Aspects of Your Main Goal Makes You Feel. . .

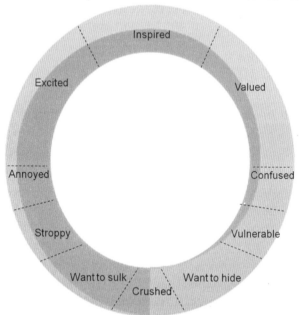

**Being open to feedback**

We know little really about what makes us do things, so we can't afford to be complacent about our self-awareness. The best context for self-reflection is conversation. This is where we discover what people think of us. *The degree to which we are open determines the impact of any feedback.*

In any effective partnership, both parties must be able to feedback issues concerning the relationship. Other people's views come with their own biases but they offer a counter balance to any bias inherent in our own perceptions. A two-way dynamic process, where partners impact on one another's morale and well-being, is essential for effective leadership, parenting or teaching.

The website accompanying this book provides free resources for garnering insights into others' perceptions of us. Leaders use the *leader* profile, teachers should use the *inspire-ring* profile and parents use the *parenting* profile. The profiles give impartial feedback in the form of a personal chart, allowing a structured consideration of our strengths and issues in relation to others. They also prime us to notice how we relate to other people and how others relate to us.

Using the leading, parenting and teaching styles helps us to analyse our behaviour in a non-judgemental and non-threatening way. The chart allows us to compare our 'good day' and 'bad day' styles. The profile also lets us see how we change from one situation to another.

We are often reluctant to seek feedback. It requires courage. Yet we also complain that we never get any feedback. Effective people seek out feedback regularly and are rewarded for doing so. A major barrier to receiving feedback is arrogance. If we see ourselves as more important than others we can dismiss the idea that others can offer useful critical feedback. If we don't check out other people's perceptions of us we are inhabiting our own fantasy world. We can't address our weaknesses if we don't know about them. Feedback from others is the only way we can know how we affect them. Asking people for their opinions about us is also a powerful demonstration of our respect, and also of our humility. Responding to feedback is an essential part of the process of forming an effective partnership.

**Tips for responding to feedback**

- Seek feedback from a variety of credible sources.

- Be open enough to accept it.

- Accept the person's perspective as valid and different from yours.

- Don't over think the other person's motives.

- Consider your emotional reaction, and what's behind it.

- Ask clarifying questions to find out what the other person actually means.

- Ask for examples.

- Check your understanding by paraphrasing the main message.

- Let go of the things you can't change and focus your energies on what you can.

Receive the feedback with gratitude and grace, reflect on it with courage and respond to it with purpose. On a cautionary note, we need to evaluate the source and validity of the feedback, find out what's valuable and decide how and whether to act on it. After all, feedback from one person is only a perspective. As Marcus Aurelius, the Roman philosopher once said, 'Everything we hear is an opinion, not a fact. Everything we see is a perspective, not the truth.' Feedback from two or three people is a pattern. Feedback from a group is likely to be as objective a perspective as we can get. The online profiles can be collated together to provide a consensus of opinion.

**Ways to explore your identity**

Consider your –
    family roots, race, gender, sexuality, nationality, language, physical characteristics,
    roles and responsibilities, relationships,
    beliefs

Consider further –

What makes you feel good about yourself?

What encourages you to be your real self? What stops you being your real self?

What puts you into a good mood?

What matters most to you?

Who or what do you identify with?

What are your strengths and qualities?

What are your shortcomings and vulnerabilities?

What are the seven most important events/ turning points in your life?

At what age did you become the person you are now? What changed?

Are there any themes running through your life?

Who has primed your identity the most? How?

Who are the people you most admire?

Who are the most significant people in your life?

What have people told you about yourself that has stayed with you?

How do people get you wrong?

What would you like to be known for?

Is there any particular reputation you fear?

What are your passions, interests, hobbies, favourite music, books, films etc?

Where do you find your inspiration?

What are you most proud of? Why?

What are your strongest commitments?

What are your big aspirations?

What gives you a sense of purpose?

What attitudes and opinions do you have that you feel most passionate about?

## CHAPTER TWELVE

# The power of priming

**How can we help others to be their best selves? We can do** this by helping them to feel good about themselves. In this way we tune into and prime their positive emotions and positive identities. We can use the four WISE principles to achieve this as each principle meets a particular psychological need and primes aspects of identity. As individuals, if we live by these principles, we will bring the best out of others.

**Warmth** – priming acceptance and security
Warmth is the best starting point for a nurturing relationship. Warmth is the thing we look for when we first meet someone. It accounts for more of our evaluation of others than any other quality. This explains why, as we saw earlier, one single instance of cold behaviour towards us can lead us to see someone as hostile.

A welcoming smile signals trustworthiness and a willingness to share. By communicating a positive attitude we make people feel welcome and accepted. Listening in a non-judgmental way and reflecting back what we think we've heard also develops a warm relationship as it shows we are there for them. We can also convey warmth by recognising individuals, using their name when we talk to them. If we offer even small gestures of support, at the right time, this can have a big impact. A key element of warmth is identifying common links with others and showing an interest in their background and favourite things. Acknowledging and celebrating important life events is affirming. Evoking nostalgia is also a powerful way to strengthen a sense of belonging. Nostalgia is an emotion that helps people to re-connect with their collective identity.

**Sharing** – priming togetherness and collective responsibility
If we hold the reins too tightly to ourselves we inhibit responsibility in others. Communicating shared responsibilities with others creates a sense of interdependence. We can prime a sense of collective identity with regular use of the terms 'us' and 'we'. Relationships of mutuality require each partner to participate actively. This involves being open to the other, their perspective and feedback. Similarly, showing concern for the other party brings an essential element of mutuality.

We can see the mutuality that grows from feeling valued in the use of humour. Respectful two-way banter, where people can give as good as they get, or are even allowed to have the last word, reflects and builds mutuality. Humour signals that we don't take ourselves too seriously. Laughter expresses an acceptance of shared responsibility and tightens group bonds. It is an uplifting and contagious emotion that creates affiliation. Robin Dunbar, the British anthropologist, describes laughter as a form of 'remote tickling'. Humour is also a good way of softening a critical message and cajoling people into changing their behaviour.

When we ask people to do something for us, providing a *reason* brings them on board. *Request* plus *reason* works. The key word *because* triggers a cooperative response, and avoids cynicism and resistance. We all like to have a sound reason and purpose for doing what we have to do. This helps to connect the task to our sense of self.

**Encouragement** – priming pride and hope
Research into the coaching of high performers has shown that coaches must encourage their interest from the very beginning. This is what hooks the performers into practising the skill. Personal interest is the reason that we develop our talents in the first place. We are more committed to a task when we are *intrinsically motivated*, when we want to do it for its own sake. Tasks that provide intrinsic motivation include those which are enjoyable, give a sense of competence, are meaningful, useful for future goals, and offer choices.

As it is not possible for everyone to be the best, encouraging people to concentrate on achieving their *personal best* is an important motivator. When jogging became popular in the 1980s, the majority had to come to terms with the fact that their performance was, to say the least, modest, compared to elite athletes or even club runners. Nevertheless, the motivation to shave even a few seconds off their personal best is more than adequate to keep fun runners driven to improve.

The verbal packaging of our message is crucial as it triggers emotions. The German philosopher, Martin Heidegger, thought 'Language is the house of being.' What we say creates what we ourselves and others feel. For example the word 'should' implies conditional worth, and is associated with failure, blame and guilt. Conversely, 'could' is associated with feelings of possibility, choice and hope. I am pleased *for* you is more encouraging than I am pleased *with* you.

We encourage when we frame the task in such a way as to

appeal to people's aspired identity. For example, an intervention that successfully made healthy eating appealing to teenagers did so by framing it as an act of rebellion. It informed teenagers about the manipulative strategies used to make junk food addictive, while portraying it as healthy.

Positively framed messages encourage hope. Doctors can tell patients that from every hundred patients who have had a particular operation, ninety were successful. Or they can say that ten failed. Which one would give more hope?

The order of any request is important. Consider the apocryphal story of two trappist monks. The first monk asked the Abbot, 'Is it OK to smoke while I pray?' The Abbot was outraged. The second monk asked, 'Is it OK to pray while I smoke?' This time the abbot was impressed. This is an example of how the order in which we introduce requests is important. The first part primes the receiver to respond in a particular way.

Praise is an important source of encouragement. However it needs to be used wisely. We have to offer praise discriminately and filter out constant overused words, such as 'good' and 'brilliant', that undermine impact. If praise lacks sincerity it can become as offensive as empty compliments or ill-considered gifts, both of which indicate that the person praising doesn't really know you. Praise can be contaminated by caveats such as 'but' and 'why'. This happens when our irritation leaks out and distorts praise into criticism. For example, 'Well done, but why can't you work like that all the time?'

It is important to distinguish between showing gratitude when requests are met, and praising something exceptional. Praise is particularly effective when it affirms that previously received feedback has been put into practice. The most useful feedback is information that allows people to judge and recognise progress, repair mistakes and redirect effort. Effective praise doesn't stop at saying 'well done' but goes on to tell the person specifically what they have done well.

People are motivated by rewards in the short-term, but in the long-term rewards can make people focus more on the reward than the job. When rewards smack of surveillance, comparison with others or manipulation, they can cause resentment. Perceptions shift from seeing behaviour as self-directed to being reward driven. People then do the minimum possible to get the reward. Once the reward is no longer available, there is nothing compelling them to work.

Encouragement hints at *who* the person could become. 'I can see you as a lawyer in court.' We are particularly encouraging when we use 'you are ...' praise. For example, 'you are a deep thinker' is more powerful than 'you think deeply'. Encouragement works best by pushing people in the direction in which they want to go. Effective leaders, parents and teachers show curiosity about their colleagues', children's or students' aspirations, interests and talents. This encourages them to play to their strengths.

Negative comments are bad for relationships. Research has shown that if one partner shows contempt at the beginning of a marriage this is the best predictor of divorce. Reducing negative comments therefore is an even more useful strategy for building relationships than increasing positive comments.

Well-being involves coming to terms with failure as much as success; both are subjective states rather than objective realities. Failure can have a bigger impact than success because it damages identity. It is also easier to instil a negative belief than a positive belief. A negative belief is also harder to undo. Allowing exposure to failure, along with support to minimise its impact, helps develop resilience in the form of a robust identity that is not threatened by failure.

Giving critical feedback constructively is one of the greatest challenges in any relationship. It's an emotional minefield. If handled badly it leads to shame and rumination, resentment and denial, or hostility. When we are giving critical feedback we are walking on eggshells. We are deep in identity country, and worse still an identity that is under threat. Because people can be so sensitive we often shy away from giving critical feedback.

However, delivered respectfully, critical feedback can have a hugely positive effect. It's worth considering who has given you critical feedback that was beneficial for you? How did they help you move forward? Critical feedback may challenge and bruise, but it can make people feel accepted and valued. It also offers the reassurance of feeling understood.

Critical feedback will be greatly enhanced by any kind of external frame of reference that depersonalises the issues and reduces the direct threat to the individual. This is where various 360 degree feedback systems can be useful or the on-line profiles, stances and styles, and the Ring charts, associated with my work.

**Tips for constructive criticism**

- Check out that the person is open to feedback.

- Begin with positives.

- Consider the person in different situations and from different perspectives.

- Acknowledge the contexts that influence the person's behaviour.

- Be honest and avoid fudging through lack of clarity.

- Avoid pity and excessive, or plastic, praise.

- Help the person reframe failure as an essential part of progress.

- Link failure with factors the individual can control such as low effort and inappropriate strategies.

- Focus on the behaviour, not the person. '. . . you tend to be domineering in staff meetings' is judgemental, but '. . . you interrupt and speak over people in staff meetings' focuses on behaviour.

- Focus on how the behaviour affects your feelings.

- Avoid 'you always' or 'you never' formulations.

- Address weaknesses that stop people from using their strengths.

- Jointly elicit a clear picture of what success would look like.

- Focus on one important piece of feedback; give small amounts regularly.

It's important to bear in mind that relationships are by their nature a double act, and when there is a relationship problem it is invariably two-way. However, the way we feel can lead us to believe that people are negative or positive. But beware thinking that because someone has made you feel bad this makes them a bad person. It's more productive to think in terms of difficult or satisfying relationships, rather than 'difficult' or 'good' people. Consider the mother who constantly complains that her twenty-five-year-old daughter expects her to do everything for her. The mother doesn't realise that the problem stems from the fact that she has always done everything for her daughter and this has perpetuated the problem. In almost all cases the person perceived as 'difficult' probably views the situation differently.

With any relationship issue it can help to ask ourselves, 'What is the other person feeling? What is leading to this? Where is my responsibility in this?' The key point is not who is at fault but 'how we can work better together?' When people get critical feedback, and can attribute difficulties to the relationship rather than just to themselves, they don't wallow in self-pity or lash out in anger. They become motivated to improve. They work on the relationship. So it is best to remember that failure isn't personal: It is relational.

**Fostering independence** – priming confidence and determination

Fostering independence starts with structure. Wisely judged boundaries enhance independence, they don't thwart it. Structure provides security by letting people know what's expected of them. Rules and routines that remain the same each day help to ground us. Predictability lets people know what is coming next and so creates a relaxed mood that enables them to take risks. Structure is like a river that carries us along in a certain direction. Ideally it clarifies the extent to which people are controlled, and how much they themselves can control. Inviting people to express their opinions is an empowering way to foster independence.

Fostering independence requires us to inject some bite into our demands. Stretch produces enjoyment when it encourages people to do something they didn't realise they could do. It evokes courage. The optimal challenge is one set just ahead of the person's skill level, one that takes them beyond their comfort zone.

Giving choice is a powerful approach to encourage independence. Decision-making lies at the heart of independence. As Dumbledore told Harry Potter – 'It is our choices, Harry, that show who we truly are, far more than our abilities.' People enjoy things more and invest more if we give them choices. Once people have made a choice the need for consistency compels them to bring their attitude in line with their choice, to convince themselves that they have made the right choice. As the saying goes – 'We make our choices then our choices make us'.

Another good way to develop someone's independence is to invite them to make a commitment which, in turn, affects how they behave. Commitment changes behaviour. If people act in a certain way they adjust their attitude to be consistent with their behaviour. Commitment to any cause generates the necessary realignment of people's attitude with their behaviour and further reinforces their commitment to the cause. Commitment is self-reinforcing, as people seek to justify their commitments and choices for, as Blaise Pascal once said 'Change people's behaviour and their hearts and minds will follow.'

CHAPTER THIRTEEN
# Knowing and growing

**We aspire to be the best we can be, particularly in the things** that are important to us. But self-fulfilment requires insight. This concluding chapter offers my key insights into insight.

Knowledge of self is not a state which we can attain. It is a never-ending process because we are always evolving. Another challenge in our quest for insight is that our perception of ourselves is subjective, and inevitably flawed. In particular, our emotions intertwine with our attitudes and blind us to how we affect others.

In this book we began our search for insight by exploring personality, the aspect of self with which we are most familiar. Insight into our personality helps us deal with both the opportunities it creates for us, and the constraints it presents. However, the conclusion of this book is that the richest personal seams to explore are our emotions and our identity. Both continually prime us to make sense of our experiences and to act in certain ways.

Subconsciously we navigate life using our emotions as our moment by moment guide. Emotions help us evaluate what is happening to us. Yet often we are unaware of our emotions and take little time to examine how we feel.

More than any other aspect of self, however, it is our identity that shapes how we feel about ourselves. Identity is the key to personal growth. What brings out the worst in us as individuals is when our identity is threatened or squashed. Personality is like the vehicle that takes us where we are going, but it is identity that maps out our direction. Successful people know the direction they are growing in. George Bernard Shaw summed it up well – 'Life isn't about finding yourself. Life is about creating yourself.'

Our identity is so unique and multi layered we could never map it onto any model. But the Ring of preferences is a frame of reference that can deepen our insight and offer significant clues about who we are. It helps us to:

■ self- reflect in an impartial and non-threatening way

■ distinguish our emotions

■ realise the source and impact of our interpersonal attitudes

■ illuminate our stances and styles

■ seek constructive feedback.

The Ring is a visual representation of the ways we balance meeting our own needs with those of others. This tension lies at the heart of our psychology. One of the most interesting, and perhaps challenging, elements that comes out of my work is how the Ring shines on humility as the route to achieving balance between status and likeability. Humility, according to Confucius, is 'the solid foundation of all virtues'. Humility keeps our perspective balanced and enables us to be receptive to feedback, acknowledge our strengths and limitations and respect others' contributions. It is extremely unfortunate that

Western culture misperceives humility as a weakness when in fact it is our finest attitude and one of our finest emotions.

It is also the case that when we feel bad about ourselves, we actually bring out the worst in others. We try to avoid such bad feelings about ourselves by over-imposing upon, over-protecting or humiliating others and by so doing we threaten or invalidate their identities and trigger defensive emotions.

When we feel good about ourselves, we are in the best position to bring out the best in others. We do so by living out the WISE principles of Warmth, Independence, Sharing and Encouragement. These principles enable us to connect with others in a way that primes their positive identities.

The greatest service we can provide for others is to partner them in the construction of their positive emotions and identities. Aldous Huxley captured the challenge – 'To see ourselves as others see us is a most salutary gift. Hardly less important is the capacity to see others as they see themselves.' People's feel good preferences and attitudes towards self and others give us important clues as to how we might prime their best selves. The benefit of priming emotions and identity is, I believe, the key conclusion from my work. If we get this right much else will fall into place. Knowing that we can learn from our emotions and that we are able to grow our identity throughout our lives, are perhaps two of the most empowering insights that we can possess. These insights are priceless gifts to live out and to share. □

# The Tree Metaphor

The main parts of the tree, shown in Figure 15, represent personality, identity, motives and emotions, as well as our aspirations and achievements. The tree, like us, has roots; it grows, changes, branches out, responds to its environment and flourishes or flounders.

■ Personality – the roots and outer canopy
The personality traits we are born with are, like the roots of the tree, foundational. In addition, personality traits are manifest in the canopy. We perceive the canopy as a whole, just as we perceive an individual's personality as a whole.

■ Identity – the inner trunk
Identity, the inner me, is represented by the inner trunk. The tree trunk is the conduit for all the nutrients of the tree and as such has to be open to influence from the environment and flexible enough to adapt to the conditions.

Our attitudes are represented by the bark of the tree that protects the trunk. This mirrors how our attitudes protect our identity.

■ Our emotions – the leaves
Our emotions are represented by the leaves of the tree. The leaves are an ever changing manifestation of the wellbeing of the tree. Our emotions also display our wellbeing.

■ Our motives – the branches
Our motives are akin to the branches of the tree, reaching out to the light and in so doing, growing and giving shape to the canopy. Branches are mainly, but not entirely concealed by the canopy.

Figure 15 The Tree Metaphor

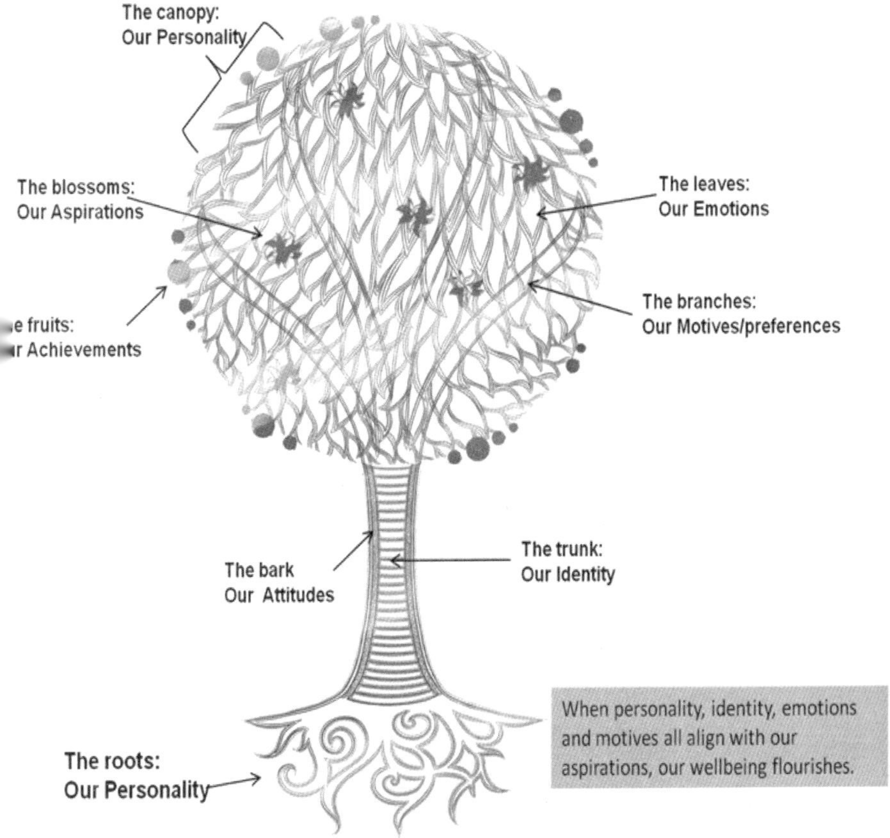

The canopy:
Our Personality

The blossoms:
Our Aspirations

The leaves:
Our Emotions

The fruits:
Our Achievements

The branches:
Our Motives/preferences

The bark
Our Attitudes

The trunk:
Our Identity

The roots:
Our Personality

When personality, identity, emotions and motives all align with our aspirations, our wellbeing flourishes.

■ Aspirations and Achievement – The blossom and the fruit

Our aspirations are represented by the blossom on the tree. The tree pours all of its energy into the blossom. Finally, the blossoms mature into the fruit of the tree, our achievements.

The condition of the tree is also, in part, the product of its environment. The tree bends with the prevailing wind and inclines towards the light. The tree is also a contributor to its environment.

# Resources

The on-line profiles can be found at:
http://www.whatmotivateslearning.com

The tools allow individuals to think about themselves as

- a student from the age of eight – the *Aspire Ring for younger learners*

- a student from the age of ten – the *Aspire Ring*

- a secondary or FE/HE student – the *Aspire Ring Further*

- a parent – the *Parent Ring*

- a team member – the *Collegium*

- teacher/lecturer – the *Inspire Ring*

- a leader – the *Leader Ring*

The profiles allow people to reflect on their relationships with and impact on others as well as others' impact on them. It helps them to express what they know intuitively about themselves but perhaps couldn't put into words. The personalised chart enables reflection and promotes discussion. A group profile can be collated to give a picture of the team ethos and also allows individuals to compare themselves to the overall group. The group profile also gives leaders and teachers a collation of their colleagues' and students' views of their style.

# Bibliography

Baggini, Julian (2015) *Freedom Regained: The Possibility of Free Will* London, Granta

Barrett, Lisa Feldman (2017*) How Emotions are Made: The Secret Life of the Brain* Boston, Houghton Mifflin Harcourt

Dweck, Carol (2000) *Self-theories: Their Role in Motivation, Personality, and Development* New York, Routledge

Epley, Nicholas (2014) *Mindwise: How We Understand What Others Think, Believe, Feel, and Want* London, Penguin

Eurich, Tasha (2017) *Insight: The Power of Self-Awareness in a Self-Deluded World* London, MacMillan

Fiske, Susan, T. (2011) *Envy up, Scorn down. How status divides us* New York, Russell Sage Foundation

Grant, Adam (2013) *Give and Take: A Revolutionary Approach to Success* London, Weidenfield and Nicholson

Kahneman, Daniel (2011) *Thinking Fast and Slow* London, Macmillan

Kashdan, Tod and Biswass-Diener, Richard (2014) *The Upside Of your Dark Side* New York, Plume

McAdams, Dan P. (2015*) The Art and Science of Personality Development* New York, Guilford Press

McCrae, Robert and Costa, Paul (1997) *Personality in adulthood: A Five factor theory perspective,* 2nd edition. New York, Guilford Press

Mercier, Hugo and Sperber, Dan (2017) *The Enigma of Reason* Boston, Harvard University Press

Mischel, Walter (2014) *The Marshmallow Test: Understanding Self-control and how to master it* London, Bantam Press

Nisbet, Richard (2016) *Mindware Tools for Smart Thinking* London, Penguin

Oakley, Barbara et al (eds.) (2012) *Pathological Altruism* Oxford, Oxford University Press

Pagel, Mark (2012) *Wired for culture: The Natural History of Human Cooperation* London, Allen Lane

Prinstein, Mitch ( 2017) *Popular: The Power of Likability in a Status-Obsessed World* New York, Viking

Schein, Edgar (2010) *Organisational Culture and Leadership* 4th edition, San Francisco, Jossey-Bass

Solomon, Robert (2007) *True to Our Emotions: What Our Emotions Are Really telling us* Oxford, Oxford Univ Press

Steele, Claude M. (2010) *Whistling Vivaldi* New York, Norton

Tomasello, Michael (2016) *A Natural History of Human Morality: Why being good is a miracle* Boston, Harvard University Press

Tracy, Jessica, L. et al (eds.) *The Self-Conscious Emotions: Theory and Research* New York, Guilford Press

Tracy, Jessica, L. (2016) *Take Pride: Why the Deadliest Sin Holds the Secret to Human Success* Boston, Houghton Mifflin Harcourt

Trivers, Robert (2011) *Deceit and Self-Deception: Fooling Yourself the Better to Fool Others* London, Allen Lane

Wright, Robert (2000) *Nonzero: History, Evolution and Human Cooperation* London, Abacus

A complete set of references is available to download from:

- www.centre for confidence.co.uk

- www.whatmotivateslearning.com

# Acknowledgements

**Writing a book is a collaborative project. I am particularly** grateful to my two main collaborators, Bob Cook and Kate Whiteley, who have supported and challenged my thinking and writing over the years. For Knowing and Growing, the team was enhanced by Tom Coulter whose painstaking attention to detail on the penultimate draft greatly improved the flow of the text.

I am also grateful to friends and colleagues who commented on early drafts and encouraged me to keep going, particularly Elaine Miller, Jude McKerrecher, Kathy Shepherd and James Vance. I have been fortunate in being able to explore the challenges of self-awareness with members of younger generations and I am indebted for the insights I have gleaned from discussions with Phillipa Brown and Hannah Brown and my sons Michael McLean and Euan McLean. I am also grateful to Michael for the tree design.

My thanks also to the young people and staff of the schools who have been particularly influential in my work at different stages, Alexandra Parade and St Blane's, Milngavie Primary, St Dominic's Primary and Aberdour Primary.

It has been a privilege to work closely with Donald Fletcher whose commitment to working with the most needy young people and expertise in web development has allowed us to create the self-reflection profiles on our website that accompany this book. Donald has worked tirelessly and patiently, resolving every challenge I have set him.

I was fortunate in the final part of my career to work with a team of wise, enthusiastic and supportive educational psychologists in the Springburn Team in Glasgow and I am grateful for all of their reflections that have informed my thinking.

Over the years I have been fortunate enough to meet with colleagues who have introduced my work into their organisations, providing me with opportunities to test out my ideas. In particular I am thankful to Christine Anderson, Michael Burke, Simon Claridge, Andrew Fogarty, David Fyfe, Derek Goldman, Gillian Graham, Roddy Henry, David Hughes, Olivia Kenneally, Morag Kerr, Ann Kirkwood, Ann Middlemiss, Ron Smith, Margaret Sutherland, Ben White and the late Iain Smith.

Many people have suggested my work has application and value beyond education. Fortunately, one of these people is Carol Craig. I am grateful for Carol's invitation to contribute to this series and for her ongoing and unstinting support for this publication. It has been a privilege to work with Carol and I have learned a great deal from her in the writing of this book. I would also like to thank everyone at the Centre for Confidence and Well-being involved in this publication, particularly Fred Shedden.

**Other books in the series**

**1. AfterNow** – What next for a healthy Scotland? | *Phil Hanlon/Sandra Carlisle* The authors of this visionary book look at health in Scotland and beyond health to the main social, economic, environmental and cultural challenges of our times. They examine the type of transformational change required to create a more resilient and healthy Scotland.

**2. The Great Takeover** – How materialism, the media and markets now dominate our lives | *Carol Craig* Describes the dominance of materalist values, the media and business in all our lives and how this is leading to a loss of individual and collective well-being. It looks at many of the big issues of our times – debt, inequality, political apathy, loss of self-esteem, pornography and the rise of celebrity culture. The conclusion is simple and ultimately hopeful – we can change our values and our lives.

**3. The New Road** – Charting Scotland's inspirational communities | *Alf Young / Ewan Young* A father and son go on a week long journey round Scotland to see at first hand some of the great environmental, social, employment and regeneration projects which are happening. From Dunbar in the south east of Scotland to Knoydart in the north west they meet people involved in projects which demonstrate new ways of living.

**4. Scotland's Local Food Revolution** | *Mike Small* Lifts the lid on the unsavoury reality of our current food system including horsemeat in processed beef products, the unsustainable movement of food round the globe, and how supermarket shopping generates massive waste. It's an indictment of a food syste that is out of control. But there is hope – the growth and strength of Scotland's local food movement.

**5. Letting Go** – Breathing new life into organisations | *Tony Miller/ Gordon Hall* It is now commonplace for employees to feel frustrated at work – ground down by systems that are dominated by rules, protocols, guidelines, targets and inspections. Tony Miller and Gordon Hall explore the origins of 'command and control' management as well as the tyranny of modern day 'performance management'. Effective leaders, they argue, should 'let go' of their ideas on controlling staff and nurture intrinsic motivation instead.

**6. Raising Spirits** – Allotments, well-being and community | *Jenny Mollison/ Judy Wilkinson/ Rona Wilkinson* Allotments are the unsung story of our times; hidden places for food, friendship and freedom from the conformity of everyday life. A fascinating look at how allotments came about; why they can make such a substantial contribution to health, well-being, community, food production, and the environment; and what's happening in other countries.

**7. Schooling Scotland** – Education, equity and community | *Daniel Murphy*
The Scottish schooling system does well for many children growing up in Scotland, but to ensure that all children get the education they deserve, a better partnership of parent, child, school, government and society is needed – one to which all Scotland can contribute and from which all children can benefit. Daniel Murphy suggests eight ways to ensure that Scottish education could be stronger and fairer.

**8. Shaping our Global Future** – A guide for young people | *Derek Brown*
Young people worry about the future world they will live in: personal futures, families and jobs. But they also worry about their global futures. The possibilities and challenges ahead appear overwhelming. This guide to human achievements and future challenges is designed to help young people consider the future their children and grandchildren will inhabit.

**9. Conviction** – Violence, culture and a shared public service agenda | *John Carnochan* Policeman John Carnochan takes us on a memorable journey of discovery as he comes to grips with violence and Scotland's traditionally high murder rate. He also gives a fascinating insight into the work of Scotland's Violence Reduction Unit and why it has been so spectacularly successful. This compelling book is not about high visibility policing or more officers but the importance of empathy and children's early years.

**10. She, He, They** – Families, gender and coping with transition | *Shirley Young* How challenging can gender transition be for both parents and siblings? A story of hope and resilience, it shows that if parents can move beyond the shock and pain of their offspring's transition, all family members can come closer together and experience life-enhancing change.

More titles are planned for 2017 and 2018.

Books can be ordered from www.postcardsfromscotland.co.uk or from www.amazon.co.uk Kindle editions are also available.